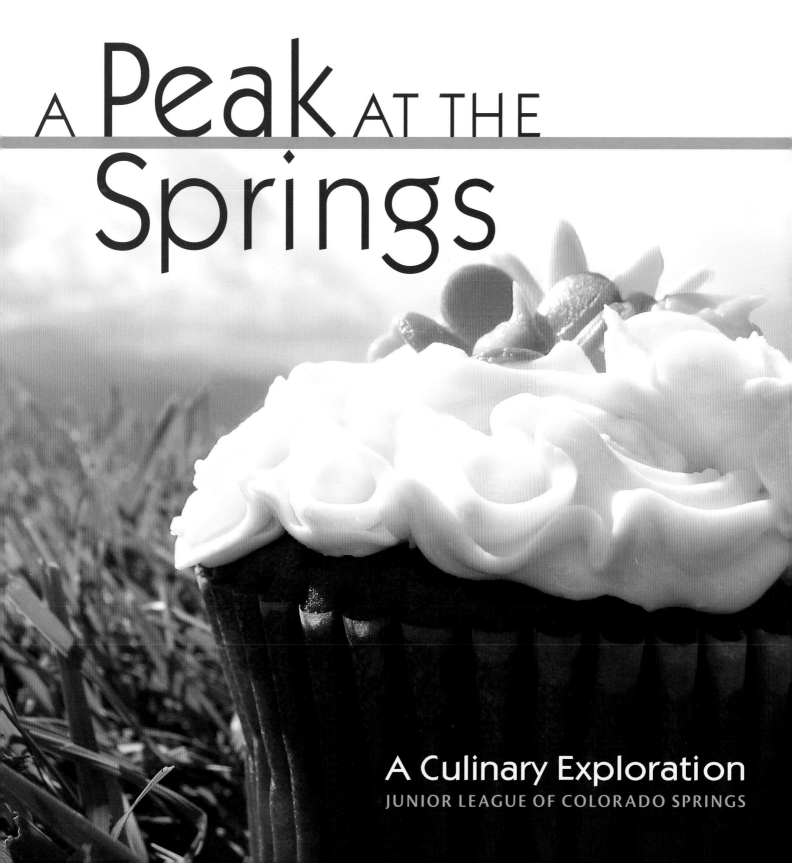

A Peak AT THE Springs

A Culinary Exploration
JUNIOR LEAGUE OF COLORADO SPRINGS

A Peak at the Springs

A Culinary Exploration

Published by
Junior League of Colorado Springs

Library of Congress Number: 2009922917
ISBN: 978-0-9822309-0-9

The Junior League of Colorado Springs is an
organization of women committed to promoting
volunteerism, developing the potential of women, and
improving the community through the effective
action and leadership of trained volunteers. Its
purpose is exclusively educational and charitable.

Proceeds from the sale of this cookbook will be reinvested
in the Colorado Springs community through the Junior
League of Colorado Springs programs and projects.

Edited, Designed, and Produced by

Favorite Recipes® Press

an imprint of

A wholly owned subsidiary of Southwestern/
Great American, Inc.
P. O. Box 305142
Nashville, Tennessee 37230
1-800-358-0560

Art Director and Book Design: Starletta Polster
Project Editor: Tanis Westbrook

Manufactured in the United States of America
First Printing: 2009
10,000 copies

Mixed Sources
Product group from well-managed
forests, controlled sources and
recycled wood or fiber
www.fsc.org Cert no. SW-COC-003334
© 1996 Forest Stewardship Council
FSC

Major Contributors

Special thanks to our major contributors for their support of A **Peak** AT THE **Springs**

Food Photography
© Dennis Lane
www.dennislanephotography.com

Food Stylist
Jacqueline Buckner
www.food4film.com

Prop Stylist
Karin Lazarus

**Cover Photograph and
Colorado Balloon Classic Photograph**
© Andrea Pacheco

**Pikes Peak Photograph, Garden of the Gods
Photograph, and back cover Photograph**
© Todd Caudle
www.toddcaudle.com

U. S. Air Force Academy Photograph
© Danny Myers

America the Beautiful Park Photograph
© Jessica Feis

The Red Door, Old Colorado City Photograph
© Bruce Thomas

A special thanks to the local chefs
who contributed recipes in support of
A Peak at the Springs.

Andrew Darrigan

James W. Davis, Jr.

Jerad Dody

Barry Dunlap

Lawrence "Chip" Johnson

Nancy Johnson

Jonathan Peterson

Alicia Prescott

Brian Sack

Greg Soukup

Cookbook Development Committee

Courtney Arnstein – *Chair*
Lauré Secker – *Assistant Chair*
Emily Boyes
Kim Feffer
Tricia Flood
Cindy Huff
Molly Kinne
Sarah Lueckman
Tracey Muterspaugh
Shannon Rowe
Helen Wilkins

2008–2009 Board of Directors

President – Joy Love
President-elect – Jennifer Clarke
Community Outreach Vice President – Barbie Walsh
Membership Vice President – Chana Kolman
Resource Management Vice President – Jenny Bender
Treasurer – Megan Harmon
Assistant Treasurer – Lisa Scott
Recording Secretary – Hartley Pohjola
Member-at-large – Tracey Johnson
Sustainer Representative – Linda Pestana

Junior League of Colorado Springs

Women Building Better Communities

The Junior League of Colorado Springs improves and strengthens our community by developing strong women leaders and passionate volunteers who support youth and family causes through fundraising, volunteering, and special events.

In celebration of its eighty-fifth year working with the Colorado Springs community, the Junior League of Colorado Springs proudly presents *A Peak at the Springs, A Culinary Exploration*. As with all of the Junior League of Colorado Springs fundraising endeavors, this cookbook is an investment in our community. Proceeds support our mission, which focuses on the health and development of women and children in the Pikes Peak Region.

Our Signature Projects

CARE Fair – Community Assistance Resource Event Fair

CARE Fair is an annual back-to-school event for uninsured children ages four through eighteen from Colorado Springs and the surrounding areas. Children receive, at no cost: immunizations and physicals, as well as dental, hearing, vision, and diabetes screenings. In addition, haircuts, backpacks, and school supplies are offered to help kids get ready for the upcoming school year.

Kids in the Kitchen

The Kids in the Kitchen initiative, which was launched by more than two hundred Junior Leagues across the country, is a response to the alarming recent increases in childhood obesity. According to the Colorado Children's Campaign, nearly 29 percent of Colorado children ages two through fourteen were considered overweight or at risk of becoming overweight. The goal of Kids in the Kitchen is to raise awareness of this issue and to help reverse the growth of childhood obesity and its associated health issues. Children enjoy learning about healthy food choices, the benefits of exercise, and how to prepare their own snacks and meals.

Fantasy Flight

Each December, children from the Colorado Springs community get the chance of a lifetime—a flight to the "North Pole" to visit Santa Claus. In conjunction with community partner SkyWest airlines, fifty children are given a boarding pass at the Colorado Springs airport for Flight One, a twenty-minute flight direct to the North Pole. Upon arrival at the North Pole, children and their families enjoy music, food, games, holiday gifts, and a visit with Santa.

Throughout its history the Junior League of Colorado Springs has addressed important community needs, launched or assisted with the formation of landmark organizations, and given more than $2 million and 1,750,000 volunteer hours to the Colorado Springs community.

Here are the projects and organizations we have been proud to support:

Active Through Advocacy

Adolescent Pregnancy Task Force

Adolescent Girls Receiving Home

Advocacy Skills Workshop

Arena Action Research Team— World Arena

Arts and Interest—Art Lecture Series

Baby Clinic

Books Bring Adventure Radio Program

Boy's Club Library

CALL—Consumer Action Line

KOAA 5 & 30 Can Help (Consumer Advocacy)

CARE Fair

C.A.S.A.

Child Advocacy

Child Care Day Nursery

Children's Action Line, Ltd.

Children's Literacy Center

Children's Wing—Fine Arts Center

Citizen's Goals for Colorado Springs

Colorado Calendar

Communities in Schools

Community Challenge

Community Enabling Fund

Community Focus Forum

Community Leadership Institute

Community Service Corps

Court Care

Creative Writing Contest Program

Crisis Care Nursery

Domestic Violence Prevention Program

Done in a Day

El Paso County Group Socialization Program

Enviro-cycle

Facts of Life Line

Fantasy Flight

Family Ties

Fine Arts Children's Theater

Golden Happenings Radio Show

Good Grief

Hope House

IRIS—Information & Referral Integrated System

Kid Esteem

Kids in the Kitchen

Kids on the Block

La Casa Contenta

Listen Up

Los Amigos

Memorial Hospital Auxiliary

Mental Health Lecture Series

Nature Resource Guide

Newborn Audio Screening

Nutrition Camp

Parenting Education/Parenting Enrichment

Parents Are Forever

Parks Projects

Pre-School for the Hard of Hearing

Public School Milk Fund

Ronald McDonald House

Safe House/MOVE

Safe Kids

The School for the Deaf and the Blind Library

School Volunteer Services

Second Chance

Shopping Service for Convalescent Soldiers

Springspree

TOP—Teen Outreach Program

Tour Guide

Town Hall Lecture Series

USO Scrapbooks

Volunteer Career Development Training

Whitehouse Ranch Nature Trail

Women and Alcohol Media Campaign

Women's Film Festival

Women's Seminar

YES! (Youth Excelling in School)

Youth Services Bureau

Contents

Explore Colorado Springs

Todd Caudle

Pikes Peak

The 14,110-foot summit of Pikes Peak is the most visited mountain in North America, and it offers many ways to enjoy its magnificence. Take a drive up Pikes Peak Highway, hike up the Barr Trail, or even ride the Pikes Peak Cog Railway all the way to the top. You will be one of more than half a million people each year who enjoy the peak in all its glory.

Two notable events that take place on the mountain each year are the Pikes Peak Marathon and the Pikes Peak International Hill Climb. If you have a fear of heights or lack endurance, travel to nearby Cave of the Winds, where you will experience jaw-dropping wonder and astonishment at its geology and adventure rolled into one. Or go to Santa's North Pole, at the entrance of the Pikes Peak Highway, where it is Christmas all year long.

When you travel to Pikes Peak, not only will you enjoy a beautiful view, but you will also find a charming shopping and cultural treat in Manitou Springs. Nine mineral springs throughout town are fed by the snowmelt of Pikes Peak. Adam's Mountain Café, Craftwood Inn, and the Briarhurst Manor are just some of the unique places to dine while you are in town.

The United States Air Force Academy

The United States Air Force Academy was signed into existence by President Dwight D. Eisenhower in 1954 and has become one of the leading military and academic institutions in the country. The first class enrolled in the academy consisted of 306 cadets, and there have been over 36,000 graduates since. Nestled into the foothills of Colorado Springs, the campus boasts state-of-the-art facilities as well as a beautiful natural landscape.

When visiting the campus, begin with the Visitor's Center, which houses exhibits, films about the institution, and a gift shop. Enjoy a scenic walk, hike, or bike ride on one of the many trails throughout the campus, and then check out Falcon Stadium, home of the Air Force Academy football team. Any day of the year, you may look to the sky to see cadets parachuting or flying. On game days, you will find crowds of fans, lots of tailgate parties, and exciting jet fly-overs.

One sight you won't want to miss is the Cadet Chapel. Dedicated in 1963, this spectacular structure is the most visited man-made tourist attraction in Colorado. Tour the chapels of four main faiths—Protestant, Catholic, Jewish, and Buddhist—and look in awe at the seventeen magnificent spires soaring 150 feet into the sky.

After an exciting day at the Air Force Academy, give your feet a rest by enjoying one of the many independently owned restaurants in the area. Go for fabulous fare at Margarita at Pine Creek or Plate World Cuisine, or head north to the Inn at Palmer Divide to dine at moZaic.

Danny Myers

Todd Caudle

Garden of the Gods

When General William Jackson Palmer purchased Garden of the Gods in 1879, he wanted it to "remain free to the public." In 1909, after Palmer's death, his children carried out his wish and conveyed the park to the City of Colorado Springs. At Garden of the Gods Visitor and Nature Center, discover how giant red rock formations were shaped. Find out about the park's unique blend of plants and wildlife from the grasslands, foothills, and mountains by taking a guided tour.

You can enjoy the park itself by driving, hiking, biking, horseback riding, or even rock climbing! Any way you decide to see its beauty, watch for well-known landmark formations like the Gateway Rocks, Balanced Rock, and Kissing Camels. You can even bring a picnic lunch, and enjoy a sunny Colorado day.

Across the street from the Visitor and Nature Center, discover an exciting living history adventure at Rock Ledge Ranch Historic Site. After your day of hiking and unique discoveries, travel to the Flying W Ranch to observe an actual working mountain cattle ranch. Located in the foothills of Colorado Springs, the ranch has specialized in authentic western food and western style entertainment since 1953. A few minutes away, you'll find The ProRodeo Hall of Fame & Museum of the American Cowboy—the only museum in the world devoted exclusively to the sport of rodeo and its star, the rodeo cowboy.

America the Beautiful Park

In 1893, while teaching English literature at Colorado College, Katharine Lee Bates journeyed to the top of Pikes Peak. She was enamored with the spectacular views, and words of a poem began to form. She completed the poem upon her return to the original Antlers Hotel in downtown Colorado Springs, and two years later it was published to celebrate the Fourth of July. We know the poem as the song "America the Beautiful."

As part of an effort to ensure the vitality of its downtown area, the City of Colorado Springs preserved a premier thirty-acre site now known as America the Beautiful Park. The beautiful, expansive park is home to the Colorado Farm and Art Market and is linked with the County Trail System, which serves as the spine in the Pikes Peak Greenway. Parents and children alike can spend hours enjoying the incredible turning fountain sculpture called The Continuum—The Julie Penrose Fountain. When children want to be creative, they can head over to the playground where interactive art and innovative equipment encourage their imaginations to run wild.

Since you will be in the downtown area of Colorado Springs, why not take a stroll down Tejon Street? In this area you will find the Colorado Springs Pioneers Museum, as well as unique shops, galleries, and locally owned restaurants like The Famous, Nosh, The Warehouse Restaurant and Gallery, Bistro de Pinto, and The Metropolitain. Enjoy the Colorado sunshine at one of the many patio restaurants and grab a microbrew at Phantom Canyon Brewing Company. To satisfy your sweet tooth, stop by Josh & John's for homemade ice cream. Just a few blocks away visit the Colorado Springs Fine Arts Center, which features nine permanent collection galleries and two traveling exhibition galleries.

Jessica Feis

Bruce Thomas

Old Colorado City

The historic district of Old Colorado City, a section of greater Colorado Springs, combines shopping, dining, entertainment, and special events into a charming and unique experience. Beautiful hundred-year-old brick buildings and tree-lined sidewalks provide the setting for more than 125 specialty shops, boutiques, and restaurants that you won't find anywhere else in the city.

Old Colorado City is the oldest city in the Pikes Peak Region, established in 1859 and designated the first capital of the Colorado Territory in 1861. It is now a treasured National Historic District.

During your fun day of shopping, visit some of Colorado Springs' independent restaurants. Locals stand in line for the fresh bread and French onion soup at La Baguette French Bakery and Café. You can also enjoy breakfast on the patio of Bon Ton's Café, homemade ice cream at the Colorado City Creamery, burgers and beer at Thunder & Buttons, or many other unique options. On Saturdays, shop for fresh Colorado ingredients at the Old Colorado City Farmers Market. From Old Colorado City, it's only a short drive to Garden of the Gods, Manitou Springs, Pikes Peak, or downtown Colorado Springs.

Outdoor Adventure

It is no surprise that Colorado Springs is home to many areas that offer outdoor experiences and adventures. From annual special events to scenic hikes through mountains and canyons, no adventure is far from the center of the city.

Memorial Park near downtown Colorado Springs is the site of The Annual Colorado Balloon Classic. Held each Labor Day weekend, the festival boasts over one hundred hot air balloons rising against the backdrop of Pikes Peak and the Front Range. During the summer months, Memorial Park also hosts one of the city's many farmers markets.

Seven Falls is sure to satisfy the nature lovers in your group. A scenic one-mile road through South Cheyenne Canyon is the entrance to this incredible waterfall, which is best viewed from the top of a 224-step stairway. For those who prefer a less rigorous adventure, there is an elevator to a spectacular viewing platform. In North Cheyenne Canyon, stop by the Starsmore Discovery Center, and then head up the canyon to find Helen Hunt Falls as well as popular hiking trails and picnic areas.

Every visitor will find something to love about the Cheyenne Mountain Zoo. You can feed crackers to the giraffes, take a ride to the top of the zoo on the Mountaineer Sky Ride, or enjoy live animal contact in My Big Backyard—and that is just the beginning! Or you can simply enjoy being 6,800 feet above sea level, overlooking the city.

A perfect dinner is a great way to end an outdoor day, and there are many great restaurants near these sites. Find unique cuisine at The Blue Star, or enjoy a microbrew at Bristol Brewing Company.

Andrea Pacheco

Appetizers AND Beverages

Spicy Sesame Hot Wings

The wonderful flavors of sesame and cayenne pepper combine in this Asian twist on hot wings.

2 garlic cloves, minced
2 tablespoons soy sauce
2 tablespoons hoisin sauce
2$1/2$ tablespoons honey
2 teaspoons sesame oil
$1/2$ teaspoon cayenne pepper
3 pounds chicken wings
2 tablespoons sesame seeds, toasted
2 green onions, thinly sliced
Black pepper to taste
Hot pepper flakes to taste

Line a 10×15-inch baking pan with foil and spray with nonstick olive oil spray to prevent sticking. Process the garlic, soy sauce, hoisin sauce, honey, sesame oil and cayenne pepper in a small food processor until smooth. Disjoint the wings and discard the tips. Arrange the wings in a single layer in the prepared baking pan. Bake on a rack in the upper third of a preheated 450-degree oven for 20 minutes, turning once. Broil for 5 to 7 minutes on each side or until crisp and golden brown. Place in a serving bowl. Add the sauce and toss to coat the wings evenly. Add the sesame seeds, green onions, black pepper and hot pepper flakes and toss to coat. Serve hot.

Serves 6

Photograph for this recipe appears on page 23.

Chicken Won Tons with Garlic Chili Dipping Sauce

These bite-size treats are worth the effort and are proof that good things come in small packages.

Garlic Chili Dipping Sauce
1 cup mayonnaise
1/4 cup garlic chili sauce
2 tablespoons rice wine vinegar
1 tablespoon sugar
1 tablespoon sesame oil
1 tablespoon soy sauce

Won Tons
3 chicken breasts, baked
1 (48-count) package won ton wrappers
8 ounces Pepper Jack cheese, shredded
1 (16-ounce) jar sliced pepperoncini, drained
Melted butter for brushing

To prepare the sauce, combine the mayonnaise, chili sauce, vinegar, sugar, sesame oil and soy sauce in a bowl and mix well. Chill, covered, for up to one week.

To prepare the won tons, shred the chicken into 1-inch long narrow strips. Line a baking sheet with baking parchment. Place each won ton diagonally on a work surface. Place a piece of chicken, cheese and pepperoncini in the center of each won ton. Roll up and twist the ends, brushing the edges with water and pinching to hold their shape if needed. Place on the prepared baking sheet with space between each. Brush with butter. Bake in a preheated 350-degree oven for 10 minutes. Turn the won tons and bake for 5 to 6 minutes longer or until golden brown. Remove from the oven and serve with the sauce.

Serves 8 to 10

Making the won tons is a little time consuming, but worth the effort. The unbaked won tons can be frozen on a baking sheet and then stored in a sealable freezer bag in the freezer until baking time. Do not thaw before baking. The sauce is also good served with vegetables.

Cherry Tomatoes with Garlic Aïoli Pine Nut Filling

These small bites of intense flavor will disappear quickly!

1 garlic clove, crushed
2 tablespoons mayonnaise
1 tablespoon fresh lemon juice
1/4 cup (1 ounce) freshly finely grated
   good-quality Parmesan cheese
1/4 cup finely crumbled feta cheese

2 tablespoons finely chopped fresh chives
1/4 teaspoon coarsely ground pepper
1/4 tablespoon pine nuts, toasted
   and chopped
1 package red cherry tomatoes
   (about 30), at room temperature

Combine the garlic, mayonnaise, lemon juice, Parmesan cheese, feta cheese, chives and pepper in a small bowl and mix well. Stir in the pine nuts.

Rinse the tomatoes and pat dry. Shave off just enough of the ends of the tomatoes with a serrated knife to create a flat bottom so the tomatoes will stand upright. Carefully hollow out the inside of the tomatoes with the tip of the knife, being careful not to pierce the skin or cut through the bottom. Spoon the filling into the tomato centers. Arrange on a serving plate and serve at room temperature.

Look for the largest cherry tomatoes you can find since you'll be stuffing them with the filling. Do not substitute light mayonnaise or mayonnaise-type salad dressing for the mayonnaise in the filling.

Serves 15

Buttery Dijon Ham Rolls

*These delicious comfort food rolls are wonderful as an appetizer on
a fall day or served on a hearty brunch buffet.*

2 packages small dinner rolls
1 cup (2 sticks) butter, softened
1/4 onion, finely chopped
3 tablespoons Dijon mustard
1 or 2 dashes of Tabasco sauce
1 pound thinly sliced deli ham
8 ounces Swiss cheese, thinly sliced

Cut each roll horizontally into halves. Mix the butter, onion, Dijon mustard and Tabasco sauce in a bowl. Spread on the cut sides of the rolls. Layer several slices of ham and one slice of cheese on the bottom half of each roll. Top with the remaining half. Place on a baking sheet. Bake in a preheated 325-degree oven for 10 minutes or until the cheese melts. Cool for 5 minutes and cut each into halves.

Serves 12

Halibut Cheeks with Pistachio-Basil Butter

Brian Sack • *Executive Chef, The Famous*

Halibut "cheeks" are succulent and meaty with a lobster-like sweetness.

Pistachio-Basil Butter
1 cup (2 sticks) unsalted butter
1 cup pistachios, toasted, shelled and
coarsely chopped
8 ounces fresh basil, coarsely chopped
Flaky sea salt to taste

Fish
1 cup apple rice wine vinegar
6 cups (12 sticks) unsalted butter
2 1/4 pounds Alaskan halibut cheeks
8 ounces baby arugula
8 ounces fresh basil
1 to 2 tablespoons favorite oil
Flaky sea salt to taste

To prepare the pistachio-basil butter, place the butter, pistachios and basil in the bowl of a stand mixer fitted with a paddle attachment. Beat at medium speed until the butter is smooth and the ingredients are evenly mixed. Add sea salt. Shape into a log if desired. Chill, covered, until serving time.

To prepare the fish, cook the vinegar in a small sauté pan until reduced by one-half. Whisk in 1 tablespoon of the butter to finish the reduction and set aside. Melt the remaining butter in a large sauté pan. Do not boil. Heat to 120 degrees. Place the fish in the butter carefully and cook for 10 minutes or until done to taste, removing the fish if needed to test for doneness. Remove from the butter.

To serve, place the fish in the center of a square serving plate. Cut the pistachio-basil butter into medallions and place on top of the fish. Drizzle the vinegar reduction over the top. Combine the arugula, basil, a drizzle of oil and sea salt in a small bowl and toss to mix. Place on top of the fish and serve.

Serves 4 to 6

*Fresh halibut is available until late September or early October.
If you can't find fresh halibut, you may use frozen fresh
halibut. You may find fresh substitutions such as Florida grouper
cheeks, Alaskan black cod, sea scallops, or Chilean sea bass.*

Palmer Park Pecans

Cinnamon and brown sugar make these tasty treats hard to resist.

3/4 cup packed brown sugar
3/4 cup granulated sugar
1/2 cup sour cream
1 teaspoon salt
1/2 teaspoon cinnamon
1 teaspoon vanilla extract
2 1/2 cups pecan halves

Bring the brown sugar, granulated sugar, sour cream, salt and cinnamon to a boil in a saucepan. Stir in the vanilla and pecans. Spread on a buttered baking sheet. Let stand until cool and then separate.

Serves 6 to 8

Pikes Peak Pecans

1/4 cup vegetable oil
2 or 3 tablespoons light corn syrup
1 quart pecan halves
Salt to taste

Heat the oil and corn syrup in a heavy cast-iron skillet, stirring to combine as well as possible. Add the pecans and stir to coat. Bake in a preheated 300-degree oven for 1 hour or until the pecans are crisp, stirring every 15 minutes. Do not overbake. The pecans will become crisper as they cool. Invert the pecans onto waxed paper and separate. Sprinkle generously with salt. Let stand until cool. Store in a tightly covered container.

Serves 8

Smoked Salmon Brie en Croûte

James W. Davis, Jr. • *Executive Chef, The Blue Star*

Your guests will be impressed when you serve these beautiful, mouth-watering appetizers.

8 ounces cold smoked	Dash of salt
Nova Scotia salmon	Dash of pepper
1 tablespoon olive oil	1 (4-inch) wheel Brie cheese, 1 inch thick
2 tablespoons chopped fresh parsley	1 sheet puff pastry
1/2 teaspoon chopped fresh thyme	1 egg
1 tablespoon chopped fresh chives	1 tablespoon water

Toss the salmon with the olive oil, parsley, thyme, chives, salt and pepper in a bowl. Cut the cheese horizontally into halves. Spread the salmon mixture over the cut side of the bottom half and top with the remaining half. Cut into quarters. Cut the puff pastry into 4-inch squares. Place a cheese wedge in the center of each puff pastry square.

Whisk the egg and water in a small bowl to form an egg wash. Seal the edges of the puff pastry around the cheese wedges, crimping the edges on the bottom side so the top of the tapa will be smooth. Brush with the egg wash. Place in the freezer for 30 minutes to harden the cheese. Place on a baking sheet. Bake in a preheated 450-degree oven for 15 minutes or until brown. Serve immediately or at room temperature.

Serves 4

These appetizers can be reheated in a
350-degree oven for 7 minutes.

Roasted Garlic and Artichoke Terrine with Lemon and Sesame Crostini

This creamy spread is a crowd pleaser!

Spread
3 (15-ounce) cans artichoke hearts
1 1/2 cups mayonnaise
2 cups (8 ounces) shredded Parmesan cheese
1/2 cup lightly chopped banana peppers
4 garlic cloves, roasted and sliced
1/2 teaspoon crushed peppercorn blend
1/2 teaspoon paprika
Salt to taste

Lemon and Sesame Crostini
1 loaf sesame semolina bread, sliced
1/4 cup olive oil
1 tablespoon lemon zest
Salt and pepper to taste

To prepare the spread, drain the artichoke hearts and squeeze out any excess moisture. Chop the artichoke hearts slightly. Place on a baking sheet. Broil for 3 to 5 minutes or until light brown. Let stand to cool. Combine the mayonnaise, Parmesan cheese, banana peppers, garlic, peppercorn blend and paprika in a bowl and mix well. Stir in the artichokes and salt. Adjust the seasonings to taste. Spoon into a 1 1/2-quart baking dish or tureen. Bake in a preheated 350-degree oven for 20 to 25 minutes or until light brown and heated through.

To prepare the crostini, brush the bread with one-half of the olive oil. Sprinkle with one-half of the lemon zest, salt and pepper to taste. Place on a baking sheet. Broil until light brown. Repeat on the other side of the bread. Turn off the broiler and let stand in the oven until crispy. Serve with the spread.

Serves 4

Crab Artichoke Dip

Fresh crab makes this artichoke dip extra special.

8 ounces cream cheese, softened
1 cup mayonnaise
1/3 cup minced onion
1/2 garlic clove, minced

1 (13-ounce) can marinated artichoke
hearts, drained and minced
8 ounces fresh crab meat, shells removed
and crab meat flaked
Bread chunks or crackers

Beat the cream cheese and mayonnaise in a bowl until smooth. Stir in the onion, garlic, artichoke hearts and crab meat. Spoon into an ovenproof serving dish. Bake in a preheated 375-degree oven for 15 to 18 minutes or until heated through. Serve with bread chunks or crackers.

Serves 8

Cheyenne Cañon Hot Pepper Cheese Ball

Pecans and hot pepper jelly give the retro cheese ball a new and tasty twist.

2 cups (8 ounces) finely shredded sharp
Cheddar cheese
1 bunch green onions, chopped
1 cup pecans, toasted and chopped

1/2 teaspoon garlic powder
1/2 to 1 cup mayonnaise
1 cup hot pepper jelly
Crackers

Mix the cheese, green onions, pecans and garlic powder in a bowl. Stir in enough mayonnaise to make the mixture stick together. Shape into a ball and place on a serving plate. Spread the hot pepper jelly on top. Serve with crackers.

Serves 20

*You don't have to stick with the classic cheese ball shape.
Try shaping into a heart for Valentine's Day, a star for July 4th, or a
football when you have friends over to watch the big game!*

Fresh Herbs and Feta Dip with Herbed Pita Triangles

A quick and easy dip that is also great with fresh vegetables.

Dip
7 ounces feta cheese, crumbled
4 ounces cream cheese, softened
1 1/3 cups mayonnaise
1/4 teaspoon fresh basil
1/4 teaspoon fresh oregano
1/8 teaspoon fresh thyme
1/8 teaspoon fresh dill weed
4 garlic cloves, minced

Dash of freshly ground pepper
Sprigs of fresh basil, thyme and dill weed
   for garnish

Herbed Pita Triangles
1 package pita bread
Olive oil for drizzling
1 tablespoon fresh thyme
Salt and pepper to taste

To prepare the dip, beat the feta cheese, cream cheese and mayonnaise at low speed in a mixing bowl until creamy. Add the basil, oregano, thyme, dill weed, garlic and pepper and mix well. Spoon into a serving bowl. Garnish with sprigs of fresh basil, thyme and dill weed.

To prepare the pita chips, cut the pita bread into small bite-size triangles. Place on a foil-lined baking sheet. Drizzle with olive oil. Sprinkle with the thyme, salt and pepper. Bake in a preheated 400-degree oven for 10 minutes or until crispy. Serve with the dip.

Serves 8

Roasted Garlic Fonduta

Barry Dunlap • *Executive Chef, Summit Catering*

*This is a nontraditional fonduta that is very forgiving and easy to
make a day or two ahead of time.*

1 garlic bulb
1 tablespoon olive oil
1 pound cream cheese
6 ounces fontina cheese
1 tablespoon Dijon mustard
1 teaspoon kosher salt

1/2 teaspoon white pepper
1 teaspoon Hungarian paprika
3 ounces spinach chiffonade
Crostini and fresh vegetables,
    such as asparagus

Place the garlic bulb on a sheet of foil and drizzle with the olive oil. Wrap the foil around the garlic. Roast in
a preheated 350-degree oven for 45 minutes or until fork-tender. Remove from the oven and cool slightly. Cut off
the top of the garlic bulb and squeeze the garlic into a small bowl, discarding the skin.

Place the cream cheese in a microwave-safe bowl. Microwave on High at 10-second intervals until softened.
Combine the cream cheese, fontina cheese, Dijon mustard, kosher salt, white pepper, paprika and spinach in
a food processor and process until blended. Add one-half of the garlic and mix well. Add the remaining garlic to
taste. Spoon into a heavy baking dish or microwave-safe dish. Warm gently in the oven or microwave before
serving. Serve with crostini and fresh vegetables, such as asparagus.

Serves 8

*Chiffonade is a technique in which herbs or leafy vegetables, such
as basil or spinach, are cut into long, thin strips. This is
accomplished by stacking the leaves, rolling them, and then cutting
across the rolled leaves with a sharp knife.*

Tailgate Party Guacamole

*Fall in Colorado means it's time to watch football and enjoy our locally grown chiles.
For this recipe, use a fresh chile such as a jalapeño, or stop by almost any Colorado Springs farmers
market and pick up some roasted chiles.*

6 or 7 Haas avocados

Juice of 1 or 2 limes

8 to 10 grape tomatoes, chopped

1 hot chile, seeded and finely chopped

2 to 4 garlic cloves

1 teaspoon sea salt

$1/2$ teaspoon freshly ground pepper

1 scallion, chopped (optional)

$1^1/2$ tablespoons chopped cilantro
(optional)

Chopped tomatoes for garnish

Chips

Mash the avocados in a bowl until slightly chunky. Stir in the juice of 1 lime and the tomatoes. Stir in the chile, garlic, sea salt and pepper. Add the remaining lime juice to taste. Stir in the scallion and cilantro. Spoon into a serving bowl. Garnish with additional chopped tomatoes. Serve immediately with chips or use as a condiment for fajitas, tacos, burritos, and so forth.

Serves 6 to 10

*Here's how to keep guacamole from turning brown: All acidic ingredients like
lime juice and tomatoes should be added to the mashed avocados immediately
to help stop oxidation—which is one of the causes of brown guacamole.
After you spoon the guacamole into a container, place an avocado pit in the
guacamole and place plastic wrap directly on the surface of the guacamole.*

Pomegranate and Champagne Cosmopolitans

These beautiful pink drinks are perfect for bridal showers and special occasions.

4 cups cranberry pomegranate juice
2¹/2 cups orange liqueur
2 cups fresh lime juice
1 cup pomegranate juice
¹/2 cup superfine sugar

1 lime, cut into wedges
1 cup pink sugar for rimming glasses
Ice cubes
2 bottles Champagne

Mix the cranberry pomegranate juice, orange liqueur, lime juice and pomegranate juice in a large pitcher. Add the superfine sugar and stir until dissolved. Chill for 4 to 6 hours.

To serve, run a lime wedge around the rim of each glass and dip in the pink sugar to coat. Add ice cubes to each glass. Fill each glass three-fourths full with the juice mixture. Top each with the Champagne and stir to mix well.

Serves 20

One-Two Rum Punch

Two kinds of rum make this punch a big hit!

3/4 cup fresh lime juice
1 cup grenadine, or less if desired
1 cup Jamaican rum
1 cup white rum
2 cups fresh pineapple juice

2 cups fresh orange juice
Pinch of fresh nutmeg (optional)
4 orange slices for garnish
4 pineapple slices for garnish

Combine the lime juice, grenadine, Jamaican rum, white rum, pineapple juice, orange juice and nutmeg in a pitcher and mix well. Chill for 1 hour or longer before serving. Garnish with the orange and pineapple slices.

Serves 8 to 10

Eggnog-tini

Your guests will ask for this on their Christmas list every year!

1 pinch of cinnamon	1 ounce rum
1 pinch of nutmeg	1 handful of ice
2 candy canes	2 tablespoons canned whipped cream
3 ounces eggnog	Nutmeg for sprinkling

Chill a martini glass in the freezer for 20 minutes. Mix the cinnamon and pinch of nutmeg together. Crush one of the candy canes into fine pieces. Dip the rim of the chilled glass into the spice mixture. Place the eggnog, rum and ice in a shaker and shake well. Strain into the prepared glass. Top with the whipped cream. Sprinkle with nutmeg and the crushed candy cane. Garnish with the remaining candy cane.

Serves 1

The Great Pumpkin-tini

Your Thanksgiving guests will ask for seconds—maybe even thirds!

1 tablespoon ground graham crackers	1/2 ounce pumpkin liqueur or
1/2 tablespoon brown sugar	pumpkin spice syrup
1/2 ounce Sylk cream liqueur	(located in the coffee aisle)
1/2 ounce Godiva white	2 teaspoons canned whipped cream
chocolate liqueur	Pinch of cinnamon
1 1/2 ounces vanilla vodka	Cinnamon stick for garnish
Ice cubes	

Chill a martini glass for 20 minutes. Mix the graham crackers and brown sugar together. Remove the glass from the refrigerator and dip the rim in the graham cracker mixture. Pour the cream liqueur, white chocolate liqueur and vanilla vodka into a shaker filled with ice and shake well. Add the pumpkin liqueur and shake. Strain into the prepared glass. Top with the whipped cream and sprinkle with the cinnamon. Garnish with a cinnamon stick.

Serves 1

Frozen Amaretto Tea

When a plain glass of iced tea just won't do, try this twist on an old favorite.

2 large tea bags
1 cup boiling water
1 cup sugar
1 (6-ounce) can frozen orange juice
concentrate, thawed

1 (6-ounce) can frozen lemonade
concentrate, thawed
3^1/$_2$ cups water
^{3}/$_4$ cup amaretto
1 bottle lemon-lime soda

Steep the tea bags in the boiling water in a pitcher to the desired strength. Discard the tea bags. Dissolve the sugar in the hot tea. Add the concentrates, 3^1/$_2$ cups water and the amaretto and mix well. Pour into a freezer container. Freeze for 8 to 10 hours or until slushy. To serve, scoop the slush into serving glasses. Add lemon-lime soda and mix well.

Serves 4

Raspberry Lemonade Slush

Use gin or rum for this refreshing summer cooler.

1 can frozen raspberry lemonade
1 lemonade can of gin
1 can lemon-lime soda

Raspberries, mint leaves or lemon wedges
for garnish

Pour the frozen lemonade into a medium bowl. Add the gin and lemon-line soda and mix well. Pour into an 8×8-inch pan. Freeze until slushy.

To serve, spoon the slush into serving glasses. Garnish with raspberries.

Serves 4 to 6

Honey Lavender Lemonade

*The sweet floral flavor of dried lavender complements the lemon and
lime citrus in this tart lemonade.*

1/2 cup honey	3 tablespoons superfine sugar, or
1/4 cup dried lavender	more to taste
2 cups boiling water	Ice cubes
2 cups fresh lemon juice	Sparkling water or lemon-lime soda
1 cup fresh lime juice	8 sprigs of fresh lavender and/or lemon or
3 cups cold water	lime wedges for garnish

Place the honey and lavender in a medium bowl. Add the boiling water and stir until the honey is dissolved. Steep for 10 to 15 minutes. Strain the lavender from the mixture and discard.

Pour the lemon juice, lime juice and cold water into a large pitcher. Stir in the honey-lavender mixture. Add the sugar and stir until dissolved. Fill serving glasses with ice and fill three-fourths full with the lemonade. Top with the sparkling water and stir to mix. Garnish with sprigs of fresh lavender and/or lemon or lime wedges.

Serves 8

Soups AND Salads

Zucchini and Watercress Soup

Use garden fresh vegetables for this lovely spring soup.

1 onion, chopped
3 garlic cloves, finely chopped
3 tablespoons butter
2 zucchini, sliced
$1/2$ teaspoon salt
$1/4$ teaspoon freshly ground pepper
4 sprigs of fresh thyme
3 cups chicken stock
1 bunch watercress, rinsed
1 tablespoon chopped fresh parsley
1 cup cream
Salt and pepper to taste

Sauté the onion and garlic in the butter in a large saucepan until the mixture begins to sizzle. Add the zucchini, $1/2$ teaspoon salt and $1/4$ teaspoon pepper and sauté until golden brown. Add the thyme and chicken stock. Cook for 20 minutes. Add the watercress and parsley. Cook for 5 minutes. Remove from the heat and discard the thyme. Purée the soup with an immersion blender. Return to the heat. Stir in the cream. Cook for 3 to 5 minutes or until heated through. Add salt and pepper to taste. Ladle into soup bowls.

Serves 4

Photograph for this recipe appears on page 41.

Three-Pepper Black Bean Soup with Avocado

Green, red, and yellow bell peppers give this southwestern soup a wonderful flavor and color.

2 tablespoons olive oil
1 teaspoon minced garlic
3 green onions, finely chopped
1 yellow onion, finely chopped
1 green bell pepper, finely chopped
1 red bell pepper, finely chopped
1 yellow bell pepper, finely chopped
1 (14-ounce) can tomatoes with green chiles
1 (14-ounce) can tomatoes with lime and cilantro
1¹/₂ cups vegetable broth

3 (14-ounce) cans no-salt-added black beans
1 teaspoon salt
¹/₈ teaspoon crushed red pepper
¹/₄ teaspoon black pepper
¹/₂ teaspoon ground cumin
¹/₄ teaspoon coriander
¹/₂ teaspoon southwest seasoning
1 ripe avocado, mashed
Juice from 1 lime
1 tablespoon chopped cilantro for garnish

Heat the olive oil in a skillet over medium heat. Add the garlic, green onions, yellow onion and bell peppers. Cook for 6 to 7 minutes or until the vegetables are softened. Place in a slow cooker. Add the tomatoes with green chiles, tomatoes with lime and cilantro, broth, black beans, salt, red pepper, black pepper, cumin, coriander and southwest seasoning and mix well. Stir in the avocado and lime juice. Cook on High for 3 hours. Ladle into soup bowls and garnish with the cilantro.

Serves 6 to 8

Mushroom Barley Soup

This flavorful soup is even better the next day!

7 cups good-quality chicken stock
1 package dried mushrooms
3/4 cup barley
1 large onion, chopped
3 tablespoons butter
3 ribs celery, sliced
2 carrots, chopped
1 tablespoon soy sauce

8 ounces mushrooms, sliced
1 1/2 cups medium-dry white wine
2 tablespoons tomato paste
1 tablespoon dried dill weed
3 bay leaves
3/4 teaspoon dried oregano
3/4 teaspoon dried basil
3/4 teaspoon dried thyme

Bring 1 cup of the stock to a boil in a small saucepan. Add the dried mushrooms and remove from the heat. Soak for 1 hour or longer. Cook the barley using the package directions, substituting the stock for the water.

Sauté the onion in the butter in a skillet until softened. Add the celery and carrots and sauté for 3 minutes. Add the soy sauce and cook for 2 minutes, stirring frequently. Spoon into a large stockpot, deglazing the skillet with a small amount of stock if needed. Add the remaining stock, barley, fresh mushrooms, wine, tomato paste, dill weed, bay leaves, oregano, basil and thyme. Bring to a boil and reduce the heat. Simmer, covered, for 1 hour.

Drain the dried mushrooms, reserving the stock. Rinse the mushrooms to remove any dirt or grit. Chop the mushrooms. Add the mushrooms to the soup. Strain the reserved stock, discarding any solids. Add to the soup. Cook until heated through. Discard the bay leaves and ladle the soup into soup bowls.

Serves 4 to 6

Roasted Potato Chowder

2 pounds potatoes	8 ounces Cheddar cheese, shredded
2 onions	2¹/₂ tablespoons butter or
1¹/₂ tablespoons olive oil	soy margarine
1 teaspoon fresh thyme	1¹/₂ tablespoons all-purpose flour
1 teaspoon fresh sage	1¹/₂ cups milk, soy milk or half-and-half
1 teaspoon freshly ground pepper	Crumbled bacon for garnish
1 head garlic	Shredded Cheddar cheese for garnish
¹/₂ tablespoon olive oil	Sliced green onions for garnish
6 cups low-sodium chicken broth or	
vegetable broth	

Peel the potatoes. Cut the potatoes into halves and place in a bowl. Cut each onion into thirds and separate. Add to the potatoes. Drizzle with 1¹/₂ tablespoons olive oil. Add the thyme, sage and pepper and toss to coat. Spread on a baking sheet. Slice the top third off the head of garlic. Drizzle with ¹/₂ tablespoon olive oil and wrap in foil. Place on the baking sheet with the vegetables. Roast in a preheated 400-degree oven for 45 minutes. Remove the garlic. Roast the vegetables for 15 minutes longer.

Bring the broth to a simmer in a large stockpot. Process one-half of the roasted vegetables with ¹/₂ cup of the hot broth in a food processor until fairly smooth. Pour into a large bowl. Squeeze the garlic pulp into the food processor container. Add the remaining roasted vegetables and ¹/₂ cup of the remaining broth and purée. Add all of the puréed vegetable mixture to the remaining broth. Heat over low heat. Stir in 8 ounces shredded cheese.

Melt the butter in a saucepan over low heat. Add the flour. Cook for 1 minute, stirring constantly. Add the milk. Cook for 3 minutes, stirring constantly. Stir into the chowder. Cook over medium heat for 10 minutes. Ladle into soup bowls. Garnish with bacon, shredded cheese and green onions.

Serves 8

*The chowder may be prepared ahead and stored
in the refrigerator or freezer.*

Butternut Squash Bisque with Crème Fraîche

Lawrence "Chip" Johnson • *Proprietor and Executive Chef,*
The Warehouse Restaurant and Gallery

Crème fraîche makes this fall soup delightfully rich.

1/4 cup olive oil	1 quart crème fraîche
2 large onions, chopped	1 cup heavy cream
4 pounds butternut squash, peeled,	1/4 cup honey
seeded and coarsely chopped	Salt and pepper to taste
1 quart water	

Heat the olive oil in a large heavy stockpot over medium heat. Add the onions and cook until translucent. Add the squash. Add just enough of the water to cover by 2 inches. Simmer until the squash is soft. Purée the soup until smooth using an immersion blender or a food processor. If using a food processor, return the soup to the stockpot. Stir in the crème fraîche, cream, honey, salt and pepper and heat over medium heat. Add additional water if needed to thin to the desired consistency. Ladle into soup bowls.

Serves 8

Purchase crème fraîche in specialty stores, or make it at home. Mix 1 quart whipping cream, 1 tablespoon sour cream and 1 teaspoon rice wine vinegar in a metal bowl. Let stand in a fairly warm place for 4 to 5 hours or until the consistency of sour cream. Store in the refrigerator for several weeks. It will thicken in the refrigerator also.

Chicken Enchilada Soup

This recipe calls for masa harina, a traditional Mexican corn flour, which may be found in most grocery stores. This soup is really quick to make and is even better the next day.

3 to 4 pounds boneless skinless chicken
Garlic powder to taste
Onion powder to taste
1/4 cup chicken soup base
3 cups chopped yellow onions
4 teaspoons ground cumin
4 teaspoons chili powder
4 teaspoons garlic powder
1 cup vegetable oil
2 cups masa harina

3 to 4 quarts water
1 (15-ounce) can chopped tomatoes
2 cups medium chunky salsa
1 (27-ounce) can chopped green chiles
1 1/2 to 2 pounds Velveeta cheese, cut into cubes
Shredded Cheddar cheese for garnish
Crumbled tortilla chips for garnish
Salsa for garnish

Place the chicken in a large saucepan and cover with water. Add garlic powder and onion powder. Bring to a boil and boil until the chicken is cooked through. Drain the chicken and let stand until cool enough to handle. Shred the chicken.

Sauté the chicken base, onions, cumin, chili powder and 4 teaspoons garlic powder in the oil in a large stockpot for 5 minutes or until the onions are soft and translucent.

Stir the masa harina into 1 quart water in a bowl until all lumps are dissolved, adding more of the water if needed. Add to the sautéed onions and bring to a boil. Boil for 2 to 3 minutes or until very thick, stirring constantly. Add the remaining water. Stir in the tomatoes, 2 cups salsa and the green chiles. Return to a boil, stirring occasionally. Add the Velveeta cheese. Cook until the cheese melts, stirring constantly. Reduce the heat. Stir in the chicken. Cook until heated through. Ladle into soup bowls. Garnish with Cheddar cheese, tortilla chips and salsa.

Serves 16 to 20

Thai Chicken and Coconut Milk Soup

Lemon grass, chili sauce, and coconut milk play starring roles in this soup.

2 cups sliced mushrooms
Olive oil or butter for sautéing
2 (14-ounce) cans coconut milk
3 cups chicken broth or stock
8 ($1/2$-inch) pieces of lemon grass
2 tablespoons fish sauce
2 tablespoons soy sauce
$1^1/2$ tablespoons minced fresh ginger
1 serrano chile or Thai chile, thinly sliced
1 tablespoon jarred garlic chili sauce
4 boneless skinless chicken breasts, thinly sliced
$1/2$ cup thinly sliced green onions
$1/4$ cup Thai basil or regular basil
$3^1/2$ tablespoons fresh lime juice

Sauté the mushrooms in a small amount of olive oil in a skillet. Combine the coconut milk, broth, lemon grass, fish sauce, soy sauce, ginger, serrano chile and garlic chili sauce in a large saucepan and mix well. Bring to a boil and reduce the heat. Simmer, covered, for 10 minutes to blend the flavors. Add the chicken and sautéed mushrooms. Simmer for 10 minutes or until the chicken is cooked through. Stir in the green onions, basil and lime juice. Ladle into soup bowls.

Serves 6

For a variation, try the soup with shrimp and sprinkle with black sesame seeds.

Slow-Cooked Tortilla Soup

The type of salsa used in this recipe determines how spicy the soup will be.

3 or 4 frozen chicken breasts
1 (28-ounce) can chopped tomatoes
1 (15-ounce) can whole kernel
corn, drained
2 (15-ounce) cans beans such as black,
pinto or kidney, drained
1 cup salsa

1 (4-ounce) can mild green chiles, chopped
1 onion, chopped
2 tablespoons lime juice
Dash of garlic salt
1 quart chicken broth
Crushed tortilla chips
Shredded Monterey Jack cheese

Place the chicken in a slow cooker. Add the tomatoes, corn, beans, salsa, green chiles, onion, lime juice and garlic salt. Pour the broth over the top. Cook on Medium for 8 hours or until the chicken is tender. Shred the chicken in the soup with a fork. Ladle into soup bowls. Top with tortilla chips and cheese.

Serves 8

White Chicken Chili

3 (15-ounce) cans Great Northern beans
8 to 10 cups chicken broth
2 garlic cloves, minced
2 onions, chopped
2 tablespoons vegetable oil
1 (27-ounce) can chopped mild green chiles
3 tablespoons ground cumin
2 tablespoons oregano

$^{1}/_{2}$ teaspoon ground cloves
1 tablespoon cayenne pepper
6 cups shredded cooked chicken
1 cup (4 ounces) shredded Monterey
Jack cheese
1 cup salsa
1 cup sour cream

Combine the undrained beans, broth, garlic and one-half of the onions in a large stockpot. Bring to a boil and reduce the heat. Simmer for 30 minutes. Sauté the remaining onions in the oil in a skillet until tender. Add the green chiles, cumin, oregano, cloves and cayenne pepper and mix well. Add to the bean mixture. Stir in the chicken. Simmer for 1 hour. Ladle into soup bowls and top with the cheese, salsa and sour cream. You may substitute fresh roasted chiles for the canned chiles.

Serves 10 to 12

Bison Ranch Chili

*Colorado bison is a flavorful and lean meat with less fat and cholesterol
and fewer calories than beef, chicken, pork, or sockeye salmon.*

1 pound ground bison
1 yellow onion, chopped
1 (14-ounce) can no-salt-added
kidney beans
1 red bell pepper, chopped
1 green bell pepper, chopped
1 (14-ounce) can diced tomatoes
1 (14-ounce) can tomatoes with
green chiles

2 tablespoons dried parsley
4 teaspoons chili powder
1 teaspoon ground cumin
1 teaspoon minced garlic
(about 2 garlic cloves)
1/4 teaspoon crushed red pepper flakes
1/4 teaspoon salt
1/8 teaspoon black pepper
2 cups low-sodium vegetable broth

Brown the ground bison with the onion in a nonstick skillet, stirring until the ground bison is crumbly and the onion is tender. Combine with the kidney beans, bell peppers, tomatoes, tomatoes with green chiles, parsley, chili powder, cumin, garlic, red pepper flakes, salt, black pepper and broth in a slow cooker and mix well. Cook on Low for 5 hours. Ladle into soup bowls.

Serves 4

Lentil Preaching Soup

5 cups chicken stock
4 cups cold water
1 pound dried lentils, rinsed
12 ounces baked ham, chopped
2 cups chopped peeled carrots
1 cup chopped celery
1 bay leaf
2 yellow onions, chopped
White portion of 3 large leeks, sliced
3 garlic cloves, minced
1 tablespoon ground cumin
$1/2$ teaspoon dried thyme
$1/2$ teaspoon freshly ground pepper
3 tablespoons vegetable oil
$1/4$ cup minced flat-leaf parsley
2 tablespoons cider vinegar
$1/2$ teaspoon salt
Crusty bread
Soft cheese slices

Bring the stock, water, lentils, ham, carrots, celery and bay leaf to a boil in a stockpot and reduce the heat. Simmer for 1 hour or until the lentils are tender. Sauté the onions, leeks, garlic, cumin, thyme and pepper in the oil in a skillet for 10 minutes or until tender. Add the sautéed vegetables, parsley, vinegar and salt to the lentil mixture. Simmer for 30 minutes to blend the flavors. Ladle into soup bowls. Serve with crusty bread and soft cheese slices.

Serves 8

Colorado Microbrew and Cheddar Cheese Soup

One of your favorite Colorado microbrews can be added to this rich cheese soup.

4 ounces bacon, coarsely chopped
$1/2$ cup chopped white onion
3 tablespoons all-purpose flour
3 cups half-and-half
2 cups chicken stock
12 ounces white or sharp Cheddar cheese, shredded
3 dashes of Tabasco sauce
$1/2$ teaspoon Worcestershire sauce
$1/2$ cup Colorado microbrew ale, at room temperature
Salt and freshly ground pepper to taste
1 tablespoon thinly sliced green onions

Cook the bacon in a large heavy-bottomed nonreactive stockpot over medium heat until limp but not brown. Add the white onion and cook until the onion is translucent and the bacon is crisp. Stir in the flour gradually. Cook for 2 minutes, stirring constantly. Add the half-and-half and stock a small amount at a time, stirring constantly to ensure there are no lumps. Bring to a boil and reduce the heat. Simmer, covered, over low heat for 15 minutes. Remove from the heat. Whisk in the cheese, Tabasco sauce, Worcestershire sauce, ale, salt and pepper. Ladle into a bowl and sprinkle with the green onions.

Serves 6

Turkey Creek Tortellini Soup

Enjoy this hearty soup after a day of skiing or hiking.

1 pound pork sausage or turkey sausage
2 (16-ounce) cans chicken broth (4 cups)
2 chicken bouillon cubes
1 (10-ounce) package frozen spinach
1 (10-ounce) can diced tomatoes
1 (10-ounce) can tomatoes with green chiles
1 garlic clove, chopped
1 (8-ounce) can sliced water chestnuts
1 (20-ounce) package tortellini with cheese
Grated Parmesan cheese for sprinkling

Brown the sausage in a skillet, stirring until crumbly; drain. Combine the sausage, broth, bouillon cubes, spinach, tomatoes, tomatoes with green chiles, garlic and water chestnuts in a Dutch oven and mix well. Simmer for 1 to 2 hours. Add the tortellini. Cook using the package directions. Sprinkle with the Parmesan cheese and ladle into soup bowls.

Serves 8

Poppy Seed Fruit Salad

This fruit salad is wonderful on a brunch menu, but also works well as a dessert served over shortcake or vanilla ice cream.

Poppy Seed Dressing
1/3 cup honey
1/4 cup orange juice
1/2 teaspoon fresh lime juice
1/4 cup canola oil
1 1/2 teaspoons poppy seeds
1/4 teaspoon salt
1/4 teaspoon Dijon mustard

Salad
1 pear, chopped
1 banana, sliced
1 avocado, sliced
Juice of 2 limes
1 (11-ounce) can mandarin oranges,
　　drained and sliced
1/4 cup dried cranberries
1/4 cup chopped walnuts or pecans

To prepare the dressing, combine the honey, orange juice, lime juice, oil, poppy seeds, salt and Dijon mustard in a jar with a tight-fitting lid and shake well.

To prepare the salad, toss the pear, banana and avocado in the lime juice in a bowl to prevent the fruit from turning brown. Combine with the mandarin oranges, dried cranberries and walnuts in a glass serving bowl. Add the dressing and toss gently.

Serves 6

Grilled Watermelon and Jicama Salad

Summer brings the joy of eating watermelon at backyard barbecues. This summer, throw some watermelon on the grill and enjoy this gorgeous salad.

Basil and Mint Vinaigrette
1/2 cup fresh lime juice
1/2 cup extra-virgin olive oil
1/4 cup balsamic vinegar
1/4 teaspoon kosher salt
1/4 teaspoon freshly ground pepper
3 tablespoons fresh basil, chopped
3 tablespoons fresh mint leaves, chopped

Salad
3 (1 1/2-inch) slices watermelon, cut from
    the center of a medium watermelon
2 tablespoons honey
1/2 cup finely chopped shallots
1 cup crumbled feta cheese
1 1/2 cups kalamata olives, pitted and
    cut into halves
1 cup cubed jicama
16 ounces watercress or baby spinach

To prepare the vinaigrette, whisk the lime juice, olive oil, vinegar, kosher salt and pepper in a bowl. Stir in the basil and mint.

To prepare the salad, lightly brush the watermelon on both sides with the honey. Place on a preheated grill rack and grill for 2 to 3 minutes per side or until the watermelon and honey have caramelized and the watermelon is light brown. Remove from the grill. Chill in the refrigerator. Cut the rind from the grilled watermelon and discard. Cut the watermelon into bite-size cubes. Combine the shallots, feta cheese, olives and jicama in a large bowl. Add the watermelon cubes and toss to mix. Pour the vinaigrette over the salad and toss to coat. Chill, covered, for 1 to 3 hours.

To serve, place the watercress on individual salad plates. Top with the watermelon salad and drizzle with the excess vinaigrette.

Serves 6

Garden of the Gods Salad

This truly divine salad is as delicious as it is beautiful.

Candied Almonds
1/2 cup almonds
4 to 6 tablespoons sugar

Garden of the Gods Vinaigrette
1/4 cup vegetable oil
3 tablespoons white wine vinegar
3 tablespoons sugar
1 tablespoon chopped parsley
1/2 teaspoon salt
1/2 teaspoon pepper

Salad
1 head romaine lettuce, torn
1/2 head green leaf lettuce, torn
4 to 6 green onions, chopped
1 (11-ounce) can mandarin
   oranges, drained
3 or 4 grilled or rotisserie chicken
   breasts, shredded
1 or 2 avocados, cut into cubes
1 Fuji apple, cut into cubes
1/4 cup dried cranberries
1/2 cup crumbled blue cheese

To prepare the almonds, cook the almonds with the sugar in a saucepan over medium heat until brown and candied, tossing constantly. Do not burn. Spread on waxed paper to cool.

To prepare the vinaigrette, whisk the oil, vinegar, sugar, parsley, salt and pepper in a bowl until blended.

To prepare the salad, combine the romaine lettuce, green leaf lettuce, green onions, mandarin oranges, chicken, avocados, apple, dried cranberries and blue cheese in a large salad bowl and toss to mix. Crumble the candied almonds over the salad. Add the vinaigrette and toss to coat.

Serves 6 to 8

Cashew Sesame Salad

Ramen noodles never tasted so good. They add a wonderful crunch to this salad.

1 cup cashews	1/2 cup canola oil
3/4 cup almonds	1 tablespoon rice vinegar
1/2 cup sesame seeds	2 tablespoons sugar
2 tablespoons butter	Salt and pepper to taste
1 head cabbage	2 (3-ounce) packages ramen noodles
8 green onions	

Sauté the cashews, almonds and sesame seeds in the butter in a skillet until light gold in color. Cut the cabbage and green onions into slices and place in a large bowl. Add the nut mixture. Blend the canola oil, vinegar, sugar, salt and pepper in a small bowl. Pour over the cabbage mixture and toss to coat. Crumble the ramen noodles over the top, reserving the flavor packet for another use.

Serves 8

Peanut and Poppy Seed Coleslaw

Peanuts add a delightful surprise to this tasty coleslaw.

1/2 cup vegetable oil or canola oil	1 tablespoon poppy seeds
1/4 cup vinegar	10 ounces shredded cabbage
2 tablespoons chopped onion	1/3 cup roasted salted peanuts
2 tablespoons sugar	Salt and pepper to taste
1 tablespoon mustard	

Combine the oil, vinegar, onion, sugar, mustard and poppy seeds in a bowl and mix well. Chill, covered, until serving time.

To serve, toss the cabbage with the dressing in a large bowl. Add the peanuts, salt and pepper and toss well.

Serves 8

Tangy Coleslaw with Blue Cheese

Blue cheese dressing gives this dish a unique twist on traditional coleslaw.

1/2 small head green cabbage	2 tablespoons apple cider vinegar
1/2 small head red cabbage	1 teaspoon celery salt
4 large carrots, peeled	1/2 teaspoon kosher salt
2 cups mayonnaise	1/2 teaspoon pepper
1/4 cup brown mustard	8 ounces crumbled blue cheese
2 tablespoons whole grain mustard	1 tablespoon chopped fresh parsley

Shred the green cabbage, red cabbage and carrots in a food processor or cut into shreds by hand. Reserve a small amount of the shredded vegetables for garnish. Place the remaining vegetable mixture in a large bowl. Whisk the mayonnaise, brown mustard, whole grain mustard, vinegar, celery salt, kosher salt and pepper in a bowl. Pour over the vegetable mixture and toss to moisten well. Add the blue cheese and parsley and toss well. Chill, covered with plastic wrap, for several hours to allow the flavors to meld. To serve, uncover and garnish with the reserved shredded vegetables.

Serves 8

The recipe can easily be reduced by half or doubled.

Three-Bean Artichoke Salad

Artichokes give the three-bean salad an upgrade.

1 (15-ounce) can kidney beans,
rinsed and drained
1 (15-ounce) can green beans,
rinsed and drained
1 (15-ounce) can garbanzo beans,
rinsed and drained
1 (15-ounce) can water-pack artichoke
hearts, chopped

$1/2$ red onion, minced
$1/3$ cup cider vinegar or red wine vinegar
$1/3$ cup olive oil
$1/3$ cup sugar
2 tablespoons dried oregano
Salt and pepper to taste

Combine the kidney beans, green beans, garbanzo beans, artichoke hearts and onion in a large bowl. Whisk the vinegar, olive oil, sugar and oregano in a bowl. Drizzle over the bean mixture. Add salt and pepper and toss gently. Adjust the seasonings to taste. Marinate, covered, in the refrigerator for several hours before serving.

Serves 8

Black and Orange Salad

Greg Soukup • *Chef/Owner, Blue Sage Creative Catering Solutions*

1 tablespoon chopped fresh
Italian parsley
1 tablespoon chopped fresh cilantro
1 teaspoon cumin
1 teaspoon paprika
1 tablespoon lemon juice
2 tablespoons olive oil

Salt and pepper to taste
3 large oranges, peeled and sliced
into rounds
1 blood orange or ruby red grapefruit,
peeled and sliced into rounds
1 cup kalamata or oil-cured olives
1 small red onion, sliced

Combine the parsley, cilantro, cumin, paprika and lemon juice in a bowl and mix well. Add the olive oil gradually, whisking constantly. Season with salt and pepper. Arrange the oranges, olives and onion on a serving platter. Drizzle with the dressing.

Serves 4 to 6

Asian Angel Hair Pasta Salad

Whole wheat pasta and turkey cutlets make this recipe light and healthy.

1 pound whole wheat angel hair pasta
6 tablespoons lemon juice
5 tablespoons vegetable oil
$1/4$ cup soy sauce
3 tablespoons fresh parsley
3 tablespoons sesame seed oil
2 teaspoons sugar
5 garlic cloves, pressed

2 tablespoons sesame seed oil
1 pound turkey or chicken cutlets, cut
    into 1-inch pieces
8 ounces snow peas
3 carrots, julienned
1 tablespoon water
$1/4$ cup soy sauce

Cook the pasta using the package directions, omitting the salt. Drain and rinse in cold water. Place in a large bowl. Combine the lemon juice, vegetable oil, $1/4$ cup soy sauce, the parsley, 3 tablespoons sesame seed oil, the sugar and garlic in a small bowl and mix well. Pour over the pasta and toss well. Chill for 30 minutes.

Heat 2 tablespoons sesame seed oil in a skillet. Add the turkey and sauté until cooked through. Add the snow peas, carrots and water. Cook until the vegetables are bright in color. Stir in $1/4$ cup soy sauce. Spoon over the pasta and toss to coat. Serve hot or cold.

Serves 4

*Serve as a cold side salad, or add more turkey and
vegetables and serve warm as a main dish.*

Tarragon Chicken Salad

The delicate flavor of tarragon with its hints of anise is a delightful addition to chicken salad. It is even better the next day.

4 to 6 pounds chicken breasts
1 teaspoon garlic powder
1 teaspoon onion powder
1 to 2 pounds red seedless grapes, sliced if needed

5 to 6 ribs celery, chopped
2 tablespoons celery salt
Sea salt and cracked pepper to taste
2 to 3 cups mayonnaise
6 to 8 tablespoons dried tarragon

Place the chicken in a large stockpot. Cover with water and add the garlic powder and onion powder. Bring to a boil and cook for 25 to 30 minutes or until the chicken is cooked through. Drain the chicken. Shred the chicken in the stockpot. Add the grapes, celery, celery salt, sea salt and pepper and mix well. Add enough mayonnaise to reach the desired consistency. Add the tarragon. Spoon into a serving bowl to serve.

Serves 8 to 10

Waldorf Chicken Salad

This chicken salad is also delicious served in pita pockets or between two slices of hearty bread.

2 Red Delicious apples or Gala apples
2 tablespoons lemon juice
2 cups chopped cooked chicken
2 cups seedless grapes, cut into halves
1 cup pecans or walnuts, coarsely chopped

1 cup chopped celery
4 ounces light sour cream
2 tablespoons light mayonnaise
$1/4$ teaspoon salt
$1/4$ teaspoon freshly ground pepper
Lettuce leaves

Toss the apples with the lemon juice in a large bowl to coat. Add the chicken, grapes, pecans, celery, sour cream, mayonnaise, salt and pepper and mix well. Spoon onto lettuce leaves to serve.

Serves 6

Main Courses

Lamb and Vegetable Stew with Whole Wheat Couscous

Marinated vegetables and lamb give this stew its amazing flavor.

1 cup extra-virgin olive oil
$1/2$ cup dry white wine
3 tablespoons thyme, minced
2 tablespoons balsamic vinegar
6 garlic cloves, crushed
2 teaspoons sea salt or kosher salt
1 teaspoon freshly ground pepper
2 pounds boneless leg of lamb,
   cut into $1^1/2$-inch pieces
8 ounces cremini or miniature
   portobello mushrooms
1 large red onion, chopped

1 pint grape tomatoes
2 to 4 zucchini or yellow squash
2 tablespoons chopped fresh mint
2 garlic cloves, minced
2 tablespoons minced flat-leaf parsley
   or cilantro
1 teaspoon fresh lemon zest
1 teaspoon fresh lemon juice
$1^1/2$ cups chicken broth
1 tablespoon butter or olive oil
$1^1/3$ cups whole wheat couscous

Whisk the olive oil, wine, thyme, vinegar, crushed garlic, sea salt and pepper in a bowl to make a marinade. Pour one-half of the marinade over the lamb in a sealable plastic bag and seal. Place the mushrooms, onion, tomatoes and zucchini in a sealable plastic bag. Add the remaining marinade and seal. Marinate the lamb in the refrigerator for 4 to 6 hours. Marinate the vegetables in the refrigerator for 3 to 4 hours.

Mix the mint, minced garlic, parsley, lemon zest and lemon juice in a small bowl to make a gremolata. Chill, covered, until serving time.

Place the vegetables with the marinade in a baking dish. Bake in a preheated 350-degree oven for 30 to 40 minutes or until the onion and zucchini are tender. Drain the lamb, discarding the marinade. Add the lamb to the baked vegetables. Bake for 10 to 15 minutes or until the lamb tests done, stirring frequently to keep the lamb moist.

Bring the broth and butter to a boil in a saucepan over medium heat. Stir in the couscous. Cover and remove from the heat. Let stand until the liquid is absorbed.

To serve, spoon the couscous onto serving plates and top with the lamb and vegetable mixture. Garnish with the mint gremolata.

Serves 4 to 6

Photograph for this recipe appears on page 63.

Pomegranate Lacquered Colorado Lamb Loin with Sunchoke Purée

Andrew Darrigan • *Executive Chef/Owner, Food Designers*

Sunchokes, also known as Jerusalem artichokes, highlight Colorado lamb—the best lamb you can find anywhere.

8 ounces pomegranate molasses
1 pound lamb loin
Salt and pepper to taste
1/2 pound sunchokes
2 lemons, cut into halves
1/3 cup extra-virgin olive oil
1/3 cup olive oil
Small micro greens mix for garnish

To prepare the lamb, line a half-sheet baking pan with baking parchment. Place a wire rack in the prepared pan. Reserve 4 teaspoons of the molasses for garnish. Brush the lamb with the remaining molasses and sprinkle with salt and pepper. Place on the wire rack. Roast in a preheated 375-degree oven for 15 minutes or to 135 degrees on a meat thermometer. Remove from the oven and tent with foil. Let stand for 15 to 20 minutes or to 145 degrees on a meat thermometer for medium-rare.

Boil the sunchokes with the juiced lemon halves in salted water in a saucepan until a paring knife inserted in the sunchokes comes out clean. Drain in a colander, reserving the cooking liquid and discarding the lemon halves. Process the sunchokes at high speed in a blender until puréed. Add enough of the reserved liquid and the olive oil to achieve the desired consistency, blending constantly.

To serve, place 3 ounces of the sunchoke purée in the center of each serving plate. Cut a 4-ounce slice of lamb and place cut side up on top of the purée on each plate. Spoon a teaspoon of the reserved molasses on top, down the side and around each plate. Garnish with the micro greens mix.

Serves 4

Maple Bison au Poivre

Lawrence "Chip" Johnson • *Proprietor and Executive Chef,*
The Warehouse Restaurant and Gallery

Flambé your way to an impressive meal featuring Colorado bison.

4 (6-ounce) bison tenderloin fillets
1/2 teaspoon kosher salt
2 teaspoons crushed peppercorn medley
1 tablespoon butter
1 teaspoon finely chopped shallots
1/4 cup Cognac
2 tablespoons maple syrup
3 tablespoons chutney
1/4 cup veal demi-glace
2 tablespoons heavy cream

Sprinkle the bison with the kosher salt and peppercorn medley. Melt the butter in a sauté pan. Add the shallots and sauté until tender. Add the bison and cook to the desired degree of doneness. Remove from the heat. Add the Cognac and ignite with a long match to flambé. Let the flames subside. Stir in the maple syrup, chutney, demi-glace and cream. Remove the bison from the pan. Heat the sauce until reduced to the desired consistency. Spoon over the bison and serve.

Serves 4

If you don't have time to make your own demi-glace,
you can buy veal demi-glace in specialty food stores,
some supermarkets, or online.

Italian Stuffed Meat Loaf

This decadent rolled meat loaf, when sliced, is beautiful enough for special occasions.

1 pound ground bison or lean ground beef
1 pound lean ground pork or pork sausage
1$\frac{1}{2}$ cups bread crumbs
2 cups (8 ounces) grated pecorino or Parmesan cheese
3 eggs, beaten
8 ounces fresh spinach
1 small jar roasted red peppers, drained
8 slices prosciutto or ham
8 slices mozzarella cheese
1 small onion, chopped
1 teaspoon dried basil
1 teaspoon dried oregano
1 teaspoon dried rosemary
$\frac{1}{4}$ cup olive oil

Combine the ground bison, ground pork, bread crumbs, pecorino cheese and eggs in a bowl and mix well. Shape into a rectangle about $\frac{1}{2}$ inch thick on waxed paper. Layer the spinach, roasted red peppers, prosciutto, mozzarella cheese, onion, basil, oregano and rosemary in the center of the rectangle. Using the waxed paper, roll up tightly to form a loaf. Place on an oiled rimmed baking sheet or in a baking dish. Pour the olive oil over the loaf. Bake in a preheated 400-degree oven for 1 hour or to 165 degrees on a meat thermometer. You may substitute sun-dried tomatoes for the roasted red peppers, if desired.

Serves 6 to 8

Stuffed Beef Tenderloin Fillet

James W. Davis, Jr. • *Executive Chef, The Blue Star*

*A slice of bacon wrapped around the steak and secured with a wooden pick will
impart extra flavor and help hold the stuffing in the steak.*

4 (7-ounce) fillets of beef tenderloin
1 tablespoon butter
$^1/_2$ cup coarsely chopped porcini mushrooms
1 shallot, minced
1 splash of red wine
Salt and pepper to taste
4 ounces Gorgonzola cheese, crumbled
2 tablespoons olive oil
4 slices bacon (optional)

Cut a $^1/_2$-inch slice in the side of each fillet with a sharp knife, moving the knife back and forth inside to form a pocket. The opening needs to be small so the stuffing will remain inside while grilling.

Melt the butter in a sauté pan. Add the mushrooms and shallot. Cook until the shallot is translucent. Add the wine, stirring to deglaze the skillet. Add salt and pepper. Stuff one-fourth of the filling and one-fourth of the cheese into each fillet, being sure to distribute evenly. Rub the olive oil on the outside of each fillet and sprinkle lightly with salt and pepper. Place on a grill rack. Grill for 4 minutes on each side or to the desired degree of doneness.

Serves 4

*Stuffed steaks cook faster than unstuffed ones, so getting an
accurate temperature reading can be tricky.*

Mexican Pot Roast Tacos

The tender shredded beef would also be great in burritos.

1 (3- to 5-pound) pot roast
1 large can diced tomatoes, drained
1 onion, chopped
1 (4-ounce) can diced green chiles
1 teaspoon garlic powder
1/2 teaspoon oregano

Salt and pepper to taste
1 (10-count) package flour tortillas
4 cups (16 ounces) shredded
   Cheddar cheese
2 cups sour cream

Place the beef in a slow cooker and add just enough water to cover. Cook on Low for 4 to 5 hours or until tender and cooked through. Remove the beef and shred. Return to the slow cooker. Add the tomatoes, onion, green chiles, garlic powder, oregano, salt and pepper. Cook on Low for 1 hour. Serve on the tortillas with the cheese and sour cream.

Serves 8

Colorado's Best Burger

These really are Colorado's best burgers. To enjoy as a Colorado Slopper, serve open-face and smothered in red or green chile.

8 ounces bacon
2 pounds ground beef or bison
8 ounces sharp Cheddar cheese, shredded
1/2 cup finely chopped red onion

2 jalapeño chiles, finely chopped
2 garlic cloves, minced
1 teaspoon sea salt
1 teaspoon freshly ground pepper

Cut the bacon into 1/2-inch pieces. Sauté the bacon in a skillet until crisp; drain. Combine the bacon, ground beef, cheese, onion, jalapeño chiles, garlic, sea salt and pepper in a large bowl and mix well. Shape into patties of the desired size. Place on a grill rack. Grill until the patties are cooked through, turning once. Adjust the seasonings to taste.

Serves 8

Lemon Veal Scaloppine

This lemony sauce works well with veal or chicken.

1¹/2 pounds veal or chicken breasts
¹/2 cup all-purpose flour
Pinch of salt
5 tablespoons butter
1 tablespoon olive oil
¹/2 cup chicken broth
3 tablespoons fresh lemon juice
2 tablespoons fresh parsley, chopped

Pound the veal with a meat mallet to flatten. Cut the veal into 4×4-inch pieces. Coat with a mixture of the flour and salt. Melt the butter with the olive oil in a skillet. Add the veal in batches and cook quickly until brown. Remove from the skillet and keep warm. Add the broth to the skillet. Cook for 1 minute, stirring to deglaze the brown bits from the bottom of the skillet. Stir in the lemon juice and parsley. Return the veal to the skillet. Cook for 1 minute, stirring carefully to coat with the sauce. Remove the veal to a serving plate and drizzle the sauce over the top.

Serves 4

Grilled Pork Tenderloin with Apricot Brandy Sauce

This quick and easy sauce wonderfully complements the grilled pork.

Apricot Brandy Sauce
1 (10-ounce) jar apricot preserves
1/3 cup orange juice
2 tablespoons brown sugar
2 tablespoons brandy

Pork
1/3 cup soy sauce
1/3 cup Italian salad dressing
3 tablespoons chopped green onions
1 teaspoon garlic powder
1 tablespoon rosemary
2 tablespoons freshly ground pepper
1 pork tenderloin

To prepare the sauce, combine the preserves, orange juice, brown sugar and brandy in a saucepan and mix well. Simmer for 5 to 10 minutes or to the desired consistency, stirring frequently.

To prepare the pork, mix the soy sauce, salad dressing, green onions, garlic powder, rosemary and pepper in a bowl. Place the pork in a sealable plastic bag. Add the marinade and seal the bag. Marinate in the refrigerator for 1 hour or longer. Drain the pork, discarding the marinade. Place on a grill rack. Grill over medium heat until tender and cooked through, brushing with some of the sauce during the last 10 minutes. Cut the pork into slices and place in a serving dish. Cover with the remaining sauce.

Serves 6

Wine and Rosemary Pasta

8 ounces bow tie pasta

1/2 cup extra-virgin olive oil

12 ounces each sweet Italian sausage and
spicy Italian sausage, casings removed

2 sprigs of fresh rosemary

1/4 cup merlot

1/4 cup pinot grigio

60 seedless green grapes, cut into halves

2 cups (8 ounces) freshly grated
Parmigiano-Reggiano cheese

Cook the pasta in boiling water in a saucepan until al dente. Drain and set aside. Heat the olive oil in a large sauté pan until shimmering. Add the sausages and rosemary. Cook for 10 minutes or until brown, stirring to break the sausages into medium pieces; drain well. Add the wines. Cook for 4 minutes. Add the pasta. Cook for 2 minutes or until heated through. Remove from the heat. Stir in the grapes. Sprinkle with the cheese and serve.

Serves 6

Chicken Pesto Pasta

*A blend of Parmesan, mozzarella, and asiago Italian cheeses is used in this recipe,
which tastes great served with crusty Italian bread.*

3 tablespoons olive oil

2 chicken breasts, chopped

Salt to taste

1 garlic clove, pressed

8 ounces penne

Olive oil for tossing

8 ounces fresh pesto

1 garlic clove, chopped

1 bunch cherry tomatoes, cut into halves

8 ounces crumbled feta cheese

2 cups (8 ounces) shredded Italian
cheese blend

Pepper to taste

Heat 3 tablespoons olive oil in a skillet over medium heat. Add the chicken and sprinkle with salt. Cook until the chicken is golden. Add the pressed garlic and reduce the heat to low. Cook until the chicken is cooked through. Cook the pasta in a saucepan using the package direction; drain. Mix the pasta with a small amount of olive oil and the pesto in a large bowl with a spoon. Add the chopped garlic, tomatoes, feta cheese and one-half of the Italian cheese blend and toss well. Add the chicken and pan drippings and toss well. Add salt and pepper to taste. Top with the remaining Italian cheese blend.

Serves 5

Chicken with Ginger Orange Sauce

Flattening the chicken helps it to cook evenly so no part of the chicken breast dries out while cooking. The ginger orange sauce would also work well served with fish.

1 cup orange juice	1 tablespoon cornstarch
1 tablespoon vinegar	$1/8$ teaspoon ginger
1 tablespoon low-sodium soy sauce	4 boneless skinless chicken breasts
2 tablespoons unsalted butter	1 to 2 tablespoons olive oil
2 tablespoons sugar	Hot cooked rice

Combine the orange juice, vinegar, soy sauce, butter, sugar, cornstarch and ginger in a saucepan and mix well. Cook over medium heat until thickened, stirring constantly. Place the chicken between two sheets of waxed paper and pound with a meat mallet until about $1/4$ inch thick. Sauté the chicken in the olive oil in a large skillet over medium-high heat until cooked through. Spoon over rice on a serving platter and top with the sauce.

Serves 4

Chicken and Spinach with Pine Nuts

Pine nuts or piñon nuts come from the Colorado piñon tree, a two-needled pine that grows wild in the state of Colorado.

2 garlic cloves, chopped	$1/4$ cup (1 ounce) freshly grated
$1/2$ cup olive oil	Parmesan cheese
1 bag fresh spinach	4 boneless skinless chicken breasts
$1/4$ cup pine nuts	$1/2$ cup bread crumbs
	4 slices provolone cheese

Sauté the garlic in the olive oil in a skillet over medium-high heat for 30 seconds. Add the spinach. Sauté until the spinach wilts. Add the pine nuts and Parmesan cheese. Sauté for 30 seconds or until the Parmesan cheese melts. Remove from the heat. Dip the chicken in the bread crumbs to coat. Place in a greased 9×13-inch baking dish. Spoon one-fourth of the spinach mixture on top of each chicken breast. Top each with a slice of provolone cheese. Tent with foil to prevent the spinach from burning. Bake in a preheated 425-degree oven for 25 minutes or until the chicken is cooked through.

Serves 4

Monterey Jack Chicken

You'll enjoy the taste sensation of the oozing cheese with herbs and wine.

8 ounces Monterey Jack cheese
6 chicken breast cutlets
1/3 to 1/2 cup all-purpose flour
2 eggs, beaten
1 cup plain bread crumbs
1/2 cup (1 stick) butter, melted
2 tablespoons minced parsley
1/2 to 1 tablespoon dried marjoram
1/2 teaspoon dried thyme
1/2 cup chardonnay or other white wine
Hot cooked rice

Cut the cheese into six slices or you can make them smaller depending on the size of the chicken. Place the chicken between two sheets of waxed paper and pound with a meat mallet until thin. Wrap each chicken cutlet around a cheese slice. Dredge in the flour. Dip in the beaten eggs and roll in the bread crumbs. Arrange in a 2-quart baking dish. Combine the butter, parsley, marjoram and thyme in a small bowl and mix well. Pour over the chicken rolls. Bake in a preheated 350-degree oven for 20 minutes. Pour the wine over the chicken rolls. Bake for 15 minutes or until cooked through. Serve with rice.

Serves 6

Pan-Roasted Breast of Pheasant with Vanilla and Pears

Lawrence "Chip" Johnson • *Proprietor and Executive Chef,*
The Warehouse Restaurant and Gallery

$1/4$ cup sugar	2 tablespoons minced preserved ginger
$1/4$ cup salt	Salt and freshly ground pepper to taste
1 quart cold water	2 cups dry red wine
4 large pheasant breasts, removed from the bone with shin and wing tip attached	$1/4$ cup honey
	1 tablespoon coriander seeds, toasted and finely crushed
4 tablespoons unsalted butter	2 Anjou pears, cut into $1/2$-inch-thick slices
1 cup chopped shallots	2 tablespoons sugar
Seeds from 1 large vanilla bean	2 cups hot cooked rice pilaf
$1/2$ cup dry white wine	2 tablespoons snipped fresh chives
1 cup pear cider	4 vanilla beans for garnish
1 cup heavy cream	4 chive blades for garnish

Dissolve $1/4$ cup sugar and $1/4$ cup salt in the water in a large bowl. Add the pheasant. Chill, covered with plastic wrap, for 8 to 10 hours. Melt 1 tablespoon butter in a nonstick skillet over medium to medium-high heat. Add the shallots and cook until tender. Add the vanilla bean seeds, white wine, cider and cream. Simmer for 10 minutes or until reduced and thickened to a sauce consistency. Add the ginger, salt and pepper. Remove from the heat and keep warm. Bring the red wine and honey to a simmer in a saucepan over high heat. Cook until the mixture is reduced enough to coat the back of a spoon. Remove from the heat and set aside.

Drain the pheasant. Sprinkle with salt and pepper to taste and the coriander. Melt 2 tablespoons butter in a nonstick ovenproof skillet over high heat. Add the pheasant skin side down. Cook until brown and well-seared. Turn over and place the skillet on the lower oven rack. Bake in a preheated 375-degree oven for 6 to 8 minutes or until cooked through. Carefully remove the skillet from the oven and let stand for a few minutes. Melt 1 tablespoon butter in a nonstick skillet over high heat. Add the pears. Cook just until the pears begin to soften. Add 2 tablespoons sugar. Cook until brown around the edges, stirring occasionally. Remove the pears and keep warm.

To assemble and serve, spoon the rice pilaf in the center of each hot serving plate. Arrange the pear slices around the rice. Cut each pheasant breast on the bias into four to six thin broad slices. Place on the rice. Spoon the vanilla ginger sauce and the red wine honey sauce over and around the pheasant. Sprinkle each dish with freshly ground pepper and chives. Garnish with the vanilla beans and chive blades. Serve immediately.

Serves 4

Lobster Ravioli with Saffron Sauce

*Made with won ton wrappers, these decadent ravioli could also be filled with
mascarpone cheese and butternut squash.*

Ravioli
2 large lobster tails, boiled and chopped
8 ounces mascarpone cheese
2 tablespoons lemon zest
2 tablespoons fresh parsley, chopped
Salt and pepper to taste
36 won ton wrappers
1 tablespoon salt

Saffron Sauce
1 shallot, finely chopped
1 garlic clove, chopped
2 tablespoons butter
Salt and pepper to taste
$1/4$ teaspoon saffron
$1/3$ cup heavy cream
$1/2$ cup (2 ounces) grated
Parmesan cheese

To prepare the ravioli, combine the lobster, cheese, lemon zest, parsley, salt and pepper to taste in a bowl and mix well. Place one-half of the won ton wrappers on a flat surface. Spoon 1 tablespoon of the lobster mixture in the center of each. Brush a small amount of water on the outer edge of each wrapper. Top with the remaining won ton wrappers and press gently around the filling and edges to seal. Fill a large saucepan with water and bring to a boil. Add 1 tablespoon salt and the ravioli. Boil for 30 seconds; drain. Remove to a platter.

To prepare the sauce, sauté the shallot and garlic in the butter in a saucepan for 1 minute. Add salt and pepper to taste. Stir in the saffron and cream. Bring to a boil and reduce the heat. Simmer for 2 minutes, stirring frequently.

To serve, spoon 2 tablespoons of the sauce onto each serving plate. Add the ravioli and top with the remaining sauce. Sprinkle with the cheese and serve.

Serves 4

*For a crab meat filling, mix together 2 cups lump crab meat, 1 cup
ricotta cheese, $1/2$ cup mascarpone cheese, one-half 10-ounce
package of frozen spinach, drained, and nutmeg and salt to taste.*

Shrimp Étouffée

This quick and easy meal can be served over rice with French bread and a green salad.

2 tablespoons butter
2 tablespoons all-purpose flour
1 cup chicken broth
1 tablespoon onion powder
2 teaspoons fresh thyme
$1/4$ teaspoon salt
$1/8$ teaspoon (or less) ground red pepper
$1/8$ teaspoon black pepper
1 cup sliced celery
1 cup sliced red bell pepper
2 tablespoons butter
1 pound fresh shrimp, peeled and deveined with tails removed

Melt 2 tablespoons butter in a saucepan. Stir in the flour. Cook until golden in color, stirring constantly. Remove from the heat to cool. Stir in the broth. Mix the onion powder, thyme, salt, red pepper and black pepper in a bowl. Stir into the sauce.

Sauté the celery and bell pepper in 2 tablespoons butter in a large skillet until tender. Add the sauce and shrimp. Cook for 3 to 5 minutes or until the shrimp turn pink.

Serves 4

Prosciutto and Sage-Wrapped Elk Tenderloin with Blackberry Demi-Glace

Jonathan Peterson • *Executive Chef, Picnic Basket Family of Companies*

2 (8-ounce) elk tenderloins
Salt and pepper to taste
4 fresh sage leaves
2 thin slices prosciutto
1 shallot, minced
1 garlic clove, minced
2 tablespoons olive oil
1 pint fresh blackberries
1 quart demi-glace
1 tablespoon cornstarch (optional)
1 tablespoon water (optional)
1 tablespoon chopped fresh rosemary

Season the elk with salt and pepper. Place two sage leaves on each tenderloin. Wrap each tenderloin with prosciutto and place in a hot ovenproof pan. Sear for 1 to 2 minutes and set aside.

Sauté the shallot and garlic in the olive oil in a skillet over medium heat until the shallot is translucent. Add the blackberries and demi-glace and cook until the liquid is reduced by one-half, stirring occasionally. Stir the blackberries into the sauce using an immersion blender. Stir in a mixture of the cornstarch and water to thicken the sauce if needed. Add the rosemary and salt and pepper to taste. Keep warm over low heat.

Bake the tenderloins in a preheated 350-degree oven for 5 to 7 minutes or to the desired degree of doneness. Place the tenderloins on a serving platter. Drizzle with the blackberry demi-glace. Serve with mashed potatoes and roasted root vegetables.

Serves 2

Thai Peanut Pasta

This recipe is also great with grilled shrimp or chicken.

1 tablespoon red curry paste
1/2 cup peanut butter
5 garlic cloves
1 1/2 tablespoons chopped peeled fresh ginger
1 tablespoon soy sauce
1 splash of white wine
3 tablespoons brown sugar
Juice of 2 limes
1/4 cup chicken broth
Cayenne pepper to taste
1 quart water
8 ounces vermicelli or other thin pasta
1 cup frozen peas
8 ounces fresh bean sprouts
2 green onions, chopped
1/2 cup chopped cilantro
1/2 cup chopped peanuts

Pulse the red curry paste, peanut butter, garlic, ginger, soy sauce, wine, brown sugar, lime juice, broth and cayenne pepper in a blender or food processor until smooth. Bring the water to a boil in a large saucepan. Add the pasta and cook until the pasta is nearly al dente. Add the peas and cook for 1 to 2 minutes or until the pasta is al dente. Rinse the bean sprouts in a colander. Pour the pasta mixture over the bean sprouts and drain well. Place in a large serving bowl. Add the peanut butter mixture and toss to coat evenly. Top with the green onions, cilantro and peanuts. Serve warm.

Serves 4

Green Chile Cheesecake with Papaya Salsa

Lawrence "Chip" Johnson • *Proprietor and Executive Chef,*
The Warehouse Restaurant and Gallery

This savory and filling cheesecake features a blue cornmeal crust and would
be ideal for a special occasion breakfast or brunch.

Cheesecake

1/4 cup (1/2 stick) unsalted butter, melted
1 cup blue cornmeal
1/4 cup boiling water
8 fresh green chiles, such as Anaheim
or poblano
1 1/2 cups sour cream
2 eggs
1 pound cream cheese, softened
2 tablespoons unsalted butter, softened
1 cup (4 ounces) shredded Monterey
Jack cheese
1 1/2 cups (6 ounces) shredded sharp
Cheddar cheese

1 tablespoon minced fresh dill weed
1/4 cup chopped fresh cilantro
Salt to taste

Papaya Salsa

1/2 papaya
1 garlic clove, minced
1/2 cup finely chopped red onion
1/2 red bell pepper, chopped
1 tablespoon chopped fresh cilantro
2 tablespoons rice vinegar
Salt and pepper to taste

To prepare the cheesecake, mix the melted butter, cornmeal and water in a bowl. Press in the bottom of a 10-inch springform pan. Roast the chiles and peel. Cut off the top of the chiles, discarding the seeds and ribs. Finely chop the chiles. Blend the sour cream and eggs in a food processor. Add the cream cheese and butter and process until smooth. Spoon into a bowl. Add the chiles, Monterey Jack cheese, Cheddar cheese, dill weed, cilantro and salt and mix well. Pour into the prepared pan. Bake on the middle rack in a preheated 325-degree oven for 45 minutes or until the center is set. Cool completely in the pan on a wire rack.

To prepare the salsa, peel the papaya. Remove the seeds and discard. Chop the papaya coarsely to measure about 1 cup. Combine the papaya, garlic, onion, bell pepper, cilantro, vinegar, salt and pepper in a bowl and mix well.

To serve, spread the salsa over the cooled cheesecake. Remove the side of the pan and serve.

Serves 6

Wild Mushroom Crêpes

Lawrence "Chip" Johnson • *Proprietor and Executive Chef,*
The Warehouse Restaurant and Gallery

A light hollandaise sauce or a thyme beurre blanc is particularly
nice served over these savory crêpes.

1 quart sliced button mushrooms	2 teaspoons sugar
1 quart sliced portobello mushrooms	2 teaspoons marjoram
1 quart sliced shiitake mushrooms	1 pound boursin cheese or cream cheese
2 cups coarsely chopped oyster mushrooms	1 1/2 cups all-purpose flour
1/4 cup chopped garlic	1 teaspoon salt
1/2 red onion, julienned	2 teaspoons baking powder
1 red bell pepper, julienned	1/4 cup confectioners' sugar
1 yellow bell pepper, julienned	4 eggs
2 cups olive oil	1 1/3 cups milk
1 tablespoon finely ground pepper	2/3 cup water
2 teaspoons kosher salt	Vegetable oil for frying

Combine the mushrooms, garlic, onion, bell peppers, olive oil, pepper, kosher salt, sugar and marjoram in a large bowl and toss to mix well. Spoon into a roasting pan. Bake in a preheated 375-degree oven for 35 to 45 minutes or until roasted, stirring frequently. Remove from the oven to cool slightly. Add the cheese and mix well. Chill, covered, for 8 to 10 hours.

Mix the flour, salt, baking powder and confectioners' sugar in a mixing bowl.

Add the eggs and one-half of the milk and beat thoroughly until smooth and lump-free. Add the remaining milk and the water gradually, beating constantly. Let stand at room temperature for 2 hours.

Coat a medium-hot 6-inch sauté pan lightly with a small amount of vegetable oil. Spoon 3 to 4 tablespoons of the batter into the prepared pan, tilting the pan to spread the batter evenly over the bottom. Cook for 1 to 1 1/2 minutes or until light brown on the bottom. Flip the crêpe and cook for 20 seconds. Slide the crêpe out of the pan onto a square of baking parchment. Repeat with the remaining batter, keeping baking parchment between each crêpe to prevent sticking together.

Spoon 1 ounce of the mushroom filling onto each crêpe and roll up. Arrange in a greased baking dish. Bake in a preheated 350-degree oven for 20 to 25 minutes or until the crêpes are hot in the center but are not too crisp.

Serves 10 to 15

Vegetables AND Sides

Edamame and Summer Corn

This is a fast, fresh, and easy summer salad.

6 ears of corn

2 tablespoons olive oil

Coarse kosher salt or sea salt to taste

Freshly ground pepper to taste

1 pound shelled edamame, cooked
al dente, drained and salted

30 grape tomatoes, cut into
halves lengthwise

1/2 cup finely chopped red onion

3 to 4 tablespoons balsamic vinegar

3 tablespoons olive oil

Remove the husks and silk from the corn. Place the corn in a shallow dish and coat with 2 tablespoons olive oil, kosher salt and pepper. Place on a grill rack. Grill over medium heat for 8 minutes or until the corn is plump and juicy, turning constantly. Remove from the grill to cool. Cut the corn from the cob into a large serving bowl, removing any stray silk or husk. Add the edamame, tomatoes and onion. Add the vinegar and 3 tablespoons olive oil and stir to coat. Add kosher salt and pepper to taste. Chill, covered, for 2 hours to allow the flavors to meld. Stir before serving.

Serves 6

Photograph for this recipe appears on page 83.

*For a variation, add black beans or garbanzo beans
and toss with fresh salad greens.*

Olathe Corn Soufflé

Jerad Dody • *Executive Chef, moZaic Restaurant at the Inn at Palmer Divide*

Olathe sweet corn is one of Colorado's agricultural jewels. It hails from Olathe,
a rural farming community located in Montrose County, Colorado.

10 ears of Olathe sweet corn
1 large yellow onion, chopped
1 garlic clove, minced
1 large shallot, minced
1 tablespoon extra-virgin olive oil
2 tablespoons sugar
6 tablespoons all-purpose flour
4 eggs
6 tablespoons heavy cream
Salt and pepper to taste

Remove the husks and silk from the corn. Cut the kernels into a bowl using a sharp knife. Add the onion, garlic, shallot and olive oil and toss to mix. Spread in an even layer on a large baking sheet. Bake in a preheated 350-degree oven for 20 minutes or until golden brown. Remove from the oven to cool.

Combine the sugar, flour, eggs, cream, salt and pepper in a large bowl and mix well. Fold in the corn mixture. Pour into 8-ounce soufflé dishes filling three-fourths full to allow for fluffiness. Place the dishes in a water bath. Bake in a preheated 325-degree oven for 1 to 1 1/2 hours or until the soufflés are golden brown and a wooden pick inserted in the centers comes out clean.

Serves 12

Beer and Molasses Baked Beans

Five varieties of beans make for a colorful and flavorful accompaniment to burgers or ham.

8 ounces thick bacon
2 cups chopped white onions
1 large green bell pepper, coarsely chopped
1 red bell pepper, coarsely chopped
1¼ cups barbecue sauce
1 cup dark beer
¼ cup dark molasses
5 tablespoons Dijon mustard
3 tablespoons brown sugar

2 tablespoons Worcestershire sauce
1 tablespoon soy sauce
1 (15-ounce) can butter beans, drained
1 (15-ounce) can black beans, drained
1 (15-ounce) can pinto beans, drained
1 (15-ounce) can red kidney beans, drained
1 (15-ounce) can garbanzo beans, drained
Salt and pepper to taste

Cook the bacon in a large skillet over medium heat until crisp. Remove to paper towels to drain and cool. Place the onions and bell peppers in a large ovenproof baking dish such as a Dutch oven or Römertopf terra-cotta baking dish. Whisk the barbecue sauce, beer, molasses, Dijon mustard, brown sugar, Worcestershire sauce and soy sauce in a large bowl. Pour over the onion mixture. Stir in the beans. Coarsely crumble the bacon and add to the bean mixture. Add salt and pepper and mix well. Bake in a preheated 350-degree oven for 1 hour or until the liquid boils. Cool for 10 to 15 minutes before serving.

Serves 10 to 12

Pepperoni Baked Beans

1 onion, chopped	3 (16-ounce) cans pork and beans
8 ounces pepperoni, cut into small pieces	1 (15-ounce) can crushed pineapple
8 ounces bacon, cooked, drained and crumbled	1 cup maple syrup
	1/2 cup packed brown sugar

Brown the onion in a nonstick skillet, stirring constantly. Add the pepperoni and cook until heated through. Stir in the crumbled bacon. Combine the beans, pineapple, maple syrup and brown sugar in a large bowl and mix well. Stir in the pepperoni mixture. Spoon into a 9×13-inch baking dish. Bake in a preheated 350-degree oven for 2 hours, stirring occasionally.

Serves 6

Sweet-and-Sour Green Beans

Everything tastes great when cooked with bacon and these green beans are no exception.

12 to 16 ounces fresh green beans
1/2 cup vinegar
1/2 cup sugar
3 slices bacon

Blanch the green beans in boiling water in a saucepan until al dente. Drain the green beans and set aside. Whisk the vinegar and sugar in a small bowl. Fry the bacon in a skillet until crisp. Remove the bacon to paper towels to drain, reserving the drippings in the skillet. Add the green beans and vinegar mixture to the reserved bacon drippings. Simmer, covered, for 20 minutes. Drain the green bean mixture and place in a serving bowl. Crumble the bacon and sprinkle over the top.

Serves 6

Italian Green Beans

This dish has very intense flavors that can work well with steak and game.
However, it also goes nicely with salmon.

12 to 16 ounces fresh French green beans
(do not use frozen)
Salt to taste
1 yellow zucchini
30 small cherry tomatoes or
grape tomatoes
10 to 15 kalamata olives, pitted and
cut into halves

1 (15-ounce) can garbanzo beans, drained
2 tablespoons extra-virgin olive oil
1/4 teaspoon kosher salt (optional)
1/4 teaspoon freshly ground pepper
1/2 cup fresh basil leaves
12 anchovy fillets, drained

Cut the tips off the green beans; if you are using young tender green beans, you may leave the tips on. Blanch in boiling salted water in a large saucepan until the green beans turn bright green. Do not overcook. Drain the green beans and place in a medium bowl.

Cut the zucchini into slices 1/4 inch thick. Cut each slice into halves. Add the zucchini, tomatoes, olives and garbanzo beans to the green beans. Add the olive oil, kosher salt, pepper and basil leaves and stir to coat. (The recipe can be prepared ahead up to this point and chilled for up to 4 hours. Let stand for 30 minutes or until at room temperature before continuing with the recipe.)

Preheat a roasting tray in a 500-degree oven. Place the vegetable mixture in a mound in the center of the hot tray. Layer the anchovy fillets over the mound. Bake in a preheated 500-degree oven for 8 to 10 minutes or until the green beans are al dente and the tomatoes are heated through. Remove from the oven and serve immediately.

Serves 6

You may be tempted to skip the anchovy fillets,
but please don't. They fall apart as they cook, so all
you'll notice is the wonderful smoky
flavor that goes well with the tomatoes and olives.

Warm Cabbage with Prosciutto Vinaigrette
James W. Davis, Jr. • *Executive Chef, The Blue Star*

This dish is wonderful with pork or steak.

Prosciutto Vinaigrette
4 ounces prosciutto or Serrano ham, thinly sliced
1/4 cup extra-virgin olive oil
1/2 large yellow onion, julienned
2 tablespoons chopped garlic
1/4 cup sugar
1/2 cup chicken stock
1 cup apple cider vinegar
2 tablespoons Dijon mustard
1/4 cup extra-virgin olive oil
2 tablespoons Italian parsley, chopped
Salt and pepper to taste

Cabbage
1/2 small head of red cabbage, julienned
2 tablespoons olive oil or vegetable oil
Salt and pepper to taste
4 tablespoons chopped tomatoes
4 teaspoons crumbled feta cheese
4 thin slices prosciutto for garnish

To prepare the vinaigrette, sauté the prosciutto in 1/4 cup olive oil in a skillet until crispy. Add the onion and garlic. Sauté until the onion is translucent. Combine with the sugar, stock and vinegar in a saucepan and mix well. Boil until the mixture is reduced by two-thirds to three-fourths. The vinaigrette should not be heavy. Stir in the Dijon mustard. Purée in a blender or food processer, adding 1/4 cup olive oil gradually. Blend in the parsley, salt and pepper.

To prepare the cabbage, sauté the cabbage in the olive oil in a large skillet until hot and still a little crunchy. Add salt and pepper. Add the vinaigrette and toss well. Heat for 2 to 3 minutes or until heated through. Divide among four serving plates. Top each with 1 tablespoon chopped tomatoes and 1 teaspoon feta cheese. Garnish each with a folded slice of prosciutto.

Serves 4

Stacked Basil Potatoes

These potatoes offer a unique presentation and are lovely served with steak, fish, or chicken.

6 small to medium red potatoes
Salt and pepper to taste
6 Roma tomatoes
1 package goat cheese with herbs
1 bunch basil leaves
Favorite vinaigrette for drizzling

Scrub the potatoes. Microwave or parboil the potatoes until a fork gently passes through the skin. Shave off one end of each potato so the potato will stand upright. This end will serve as the base. Cut each potato into thirds so you will have a base, middle and top. Place on foil lightly sprayed with nonstick cooking spray. Sprinkle with salt and pepper. Cut the tomatoes into twelve thin slices. Sprinkle with salt and pepper.

To assemble the potato stacks, layer each potato base with 1 teaspoon of the cheese, 1 basil leaf and 1 tomato slice. Drizzle with vinaigrette. Stack the middle portion of each potato on each base stack. Continue layering with 1 teaspoon of the remaining cheese, another basil leaf and another tomato slice. Drizzle again with vinaigrette. Top each stack with the remaining top potato portion and sprinkle with salt and pepper. Gently wrap the foil around the six potato stacks. Let stand for 1 hour to allow the flavors to meld or place immediately on a grill rack. Grill for 10 to 15 minutes or until the cheese melts. Remove from the grill and unwrap. Drizzle with vinaigrette. Let stand for a few minutes before serving.

Serves 6

Rosemary Roasted Potatoes

Bake on a metal baking sheet to achieve a crispy texture.

8 small Yukon gold potatoes

1 teaspoon salt

1 teaspoon freshly ground pepper

2 tablespoons fresh rosemary, chopped

2 garlic cloves, minced

3 to 4 tablespoons olive oil

2 tablespoons butter, cut into small pieces

Salt and pepper to taste

Scrub the potatoes. Cut into 1-inch cubes and place in a bowl. Add 1 teaspoon salt, 1 teaspoon pepper, the rosemary and garlic and mix well. Drizzle 1 tablespoon of the olive oil onto a rimmed metal baking sheet. Arrange the potatoes in a single layer on the prepared baking sheet. Drizzle the remaining olive oil over the potatoes and toss to coat. Dot with the butter. Bake in a preheated 350-degree oven for 1 hour or until the potatoes are crisp on the outside. Sprinkle with salt and pepper to taste.

Serves 4

Maple Sweet Potatoes

4 medium sweet potatoes

1/4 cup maple syrup

2 tablespoons butter

1/4 teaspoon nutmeg

1/4 teaspoon ground cloves

1 teaspoon cinnamon

Bake the sweet potatoes in a preheated 400-degree oven for 1 hour or until tender. Peel the sweet potatoes. Combine the sweet potatoes, maple syrup, butter, nutmeg, cloves and cinnamon in a bowl and mix well. Spoon into a serving bowl.

Serves 4

Fruitful Harvest Pumpkin

*The leftovers of this dish are delicious served with yogurt for breakfast, or serve as
a dessert with vanilla ice cream or whipped cream.*

1 medium pie pumpkin	1/4 cup honey
3 apples, chopped	1 tablespoon cinnamon, or to taste
2 pears, chopped	1/4 teaspoon nutmeg, or to taste
1/2 cup dried cranberries	Juice of 1 orange
1/2 cup chopped walnuts (optional)	1 tablespoon butter (optional)

Cut off the top of the pumpkin and reserve. Fill the pumpkin with hot water and let stand for 1 to
2 minutes. Pour out the water and scoop out the seeds and strings inside the pumpkin. Combine the apples, pears,
dried cranberries, walnuts, honey, cinnamon, nutmeg and orange juice in a bowl and toss to mix. Pour into
the hollowed-out pumpkin. Place the butter on top of the filling and replace the reserved pumpkin lid. Place the
pumpkin in a baking dish. Bake in a preheated 400-degree oven for 1 hour or until the fruit filling and pumpkin are
soft. Serve warm, making sure to scoop out some of the pumpkin with the fruit in each serving.

Serves 6 to 8

Baked Spinach and Sour Cream

This is a great dish to get your kids to eat their spinach.

1 (10-ounce) package frozen spinach	1 cup (4 ounces) grated Parmesan cheese
1 tablespoon grated onion	1 tablespoon all-purpose flour
2 eggs, beaten	2 tablespoons butter, melted
1/2 cup sour cream	Salt and pepper to taste

Cook the spinach and onion in a small amount of water in a saucepan until thawed. Add the eggs, sour cream, Parmesan cheese, flour, butter, salt and pepper and mix well. Spoon into a greased 1-quart baking dish. Bake in a preheated 350-degree oven for 25 to 30 minutes or until the center is set. To prevent separation, do not overcook.

Serves 4

Farmhouse Squash au Gratin

This is a good way to use the zucchini in your garden. You can also use butternut squash.

1 onion, chopped	1 teaspoon salt
1 pound yellow squash, chopped	3 shakes of cayenne pepper
1 pound zucchini, chopped	1 cup (4 ounces) shredded
2 eggs, beaten	Cheddar cheese
6 tablespoons butter	1 cup crushed butter crackers
8 ounces evaporated milk	3 tablespoons butter, melted
2 tablespoons sugar	

Sauté the onion in a nonstick skillet until translucent. Steam the squash and zucchini in a steamer in a saucepan and drain well. Mash the squash and zucchini together. Add the onion, eggs, 6 tablespoons butter, evaporated milk, sugar, salt and cayenne pepper and mix well. Stir in the cheese. Spoon into an oiled 8×11-inch baking dish. Mix the crackers with the melted butter. Sprinkle over the squash mixture. Bake in a preheated 350-degree oven for 35 minutes.

Serves 8

Three-Cheese Green Chile Zucchini Casserole

1¹/4 pounds zucchini, sliced

Salt to taste

3 tablespoons all-purpose flour

2 teaspoons baking powder

¹/2 teaspoon salt

4 eggs

¹/2 cup milk

1 (4-ounce) can green chiles or fresh roasted green chiles

8 ounces mozzarella or Monterey Jack cheese, shredded

8 ounces sharp Cheddar cheese, shredded

¹/4 cup chopped fresh parsley

3 tablespoons butter, cut into slices

¹/2 cup (2 ounces) grated Parmesan cheese

Boil the zucchini in salted water in a saucepan for 5 minutes; drain. Mix the flour, baking powder and ¹/2 teaspoon salt in a large bowl. Add the eggs, milk, green chiles, mozzarella cheese and Cheddar cheese and mix well. Add the zucchini and parsley and mix well. Pour into a greased 9×9-inch baking dish. Top with the butter and sprinkle with the Parmesan cheese. Bake in a preheated 350-degree oven for 35 minutes or until the top is brown and crisp.

Serves 4 to 6

Artichoke, Cannellini Bean and Pine Nut Couscous

*This spicy and filling couscous could be a vegetarian main course, but works well
when served as a side dish with grilled chicken, lamb, or fish.*

$1/2$ cup couscous
$1/2$ cup water
2 teaspoons olive oil
$1/4$ teaspoon dry mustard
2 tablespoons olive oil
2 or 3 garlic cloves, minced
$1/2$ teaspoon crushed red pepper flakes
1 (15-ounce) can white kidney beans or
cannellini beans, rinsed and drained
1 (14-ounce) can water-pack artichoke
hearts, drained and chopped

$1/4$ cup pine nuts, lightly toasted
1 teaspoon dried basil
1 teaspoon dried oregano
$1/4$ teaspoon sage
$1/4$ teaspoon dill weed
1 pinch of cayenne pepper
   (about $1/8$ teaspoon)
1 pinch of marjoram
Freshly ground black pepper to taste
Freshly ground sea salt to taste
1 or 2 green onions, sliced

Mix the couscous, water, 2 teaspoons olive oil and the dry mustard in a saucepan. Cover and bring to a boil. Cook until the steam begins to escape and then remove from the heat. Let stand for 5 minutes.

Heat 2 tablespoons olive oil in a skillet over medium heat for several minutes. Reduce the heat to medium-low. Add the garlic and red pepper flakes. Simmer until the garlic is golden and fragrant. Add the beans, artichoke hearts and pine nuts and mix well. Stir in the basil, oregano, sage, dill weed, cayenne pepper, marjoram, black pepper and sea salt. Stir in the green onions. Fluff the couscous with a fork. Stir in the artichoke sauce and serve.

Serves 6

Cumin and Coriander Couscous

The couscous can be served hot or cold.

2 cups couscous

2 cups organic chicken broth or
vegetable broth

1/2 cup pine nuts

1/4 cup olive oil

1 tablespoon ground cumin

1 tablespoon coriander

1/2 cup finely chopped red bell pepper

1/2 cup finely chopped zucchini

1/2 cup chopped chives or green onions

1/4 cup lemon juice

3 tablespoons sesame oil

Pinch of coarse kosher salt or sea salt

5 sprigs of fresh cilantro for garnish

Fresh peach slices for garnish

Place the couscous in a large bowl. Bring the broth to a boil and pour over the couscous. Cover and let stand until the broth is absorbed. Toast the pine nuts on a baking sheet in a preheated 350-degree oven for 2 to 3 minutes or until golden brown. Do not over-toast or the pine nuts will turn black and bitter.

Heat the olive oil in a skillet. Add the cumin, coriander and bell pepper and sauté for a few minutes. Add the zucchini and sauté for 3 minutes. Add the chives and sauté for 3 minutes. Remove from the heat.

Uncover the couscous and fluff with a fork. Stir in the vegetable mixture, lemon juice and pine nuts. Drizzle with the sesame oil and stir. Sprinkle with kosher salt. Garnish with sprigs of fresh cilantro and fresh peach slices.

Serves 6

This recipe can be made a day in advance.

Cheese Grits Soufflé

This fluffy and cheesy soufflé is a comfort food treat.

1/2 cup quick-cooking grits
1 teaspoon salt
6 cups boiling water
1 pound (4 cups) shredded sharp Cheddar cheese
3/4 cup (11/2 sticks) butter, melted
1/2 teaspoon garlic salt
1/8 teaspoon paprika
1 teaspoon Worcestershire sauce
3 extra-large eggs, beaten

Cook the grits and salt in boiling water in a saucepan for 5 minutes. Stir in the cheese, butter, garlic salt, paprika and Worcestershire sauce. Fold in the beaten eggs. Pour into a well-greased 3-quart baking dish. Bake in a preheated 350-degree oven for 1 hour or until the soufflé has risen about 1 inch above the rim of the dish and the top is golden brown.

Serves 8 to 12

The soufflé may be prepared and stored in the refrigerator for 8 to 10 hours. Bring to room temperature before baking.

Sweets

AND Treats

Pumpkin Cake with Cream Cheese Frosting

This cream cheese frosting is insanely good!

Cakes
2 cups all-purpose flour
1 teaspoon baking soda
2 teaspoons baking powder
1/2 teaspoon salt
2 teaspoons cinnamon
1/2 teaspoon ginger
1/2 teaspoon ground cloves
1/2 teaspoon nutmeg
4 eggs

1 cup vegetable oil
2 cups sugar
1 (15-ounce) can pumpkin

Cream Cheese Frosting
8 ounces cream cheese, softened
1/2 cup (1 stick) butter, softened
1 teaspoon vanilla extract
4 cups confectioners' sugar

To prepare the cake, sift the flour, baking soda, baking powder, salt, cinnamon, ginger, cloves and nutmeg together. Combine the eggs, oil, sugar and pumpkin in a large mixing bowl and mix well. Stir in the flour mixture. Pour into a greased and floured 9×13-inch cake pan. Bake in a preheated 350-degree oven for 45 to 50 minutes or until a wooden pick inserted in the center comes out clean. Remove the pan to a wire rack to cool.

To prepare the frosting, beat the cream cheese, butter and vanilla in a mixing bowl until creamy. Add the confectioners' sugar gradually, beating constantly until smooth. Spread over the cooled cake.

Serves 12

Photograph for this recipe appears on page 99.

All of our recipes were tested at high altitude. When baking at sea level, follow these rules: for every teaspoon of baking soda or baking powder called for in our recipes, increase the amount by 1/4 teaspoon. When a range of baking times is given, choose the shorter time.

Layered Lemon Pecan Cake

Raisins and pecans are hidden in the center of this lemon cake.

3¹/₂ cups all-purpose flour (1 pound)
1 teaspoon baking powder
2 cups golden raisins
2 cups pecans, finely chopped
2 cups (4 sticks) butter, softened
2¹/₄ cups sugar (1 pound)
6 eggs
2 ounces lemon extract

Grease a 10-inch tube pan with one-half butter and one-half shortening. Sift the flour and baking powder together. Mix the raisins and pecans in a small bowl. Sprinkle a handful of the flour mixture over the raisin mixture and stir to coat. Cream the butter in a mixing bowl. Add the sugar gradually, beating constantly until light and fluffy. Add the eggs one at a time, beating well after each addition. Add the remaining flour mixture gradually, beating constantly. Stir in the lemon extract. Pour one-half of the batter into the prepared cake pan. Spoon the raisin mixture over the top. Pour the remaining batter over the top. Bake in a preheated 325-degree oven for 1¹/₂ to 2 hours or until a wooden pick inserted in the center comes out clean. Turn off the oven and let the cake stand in the oven until cool. Remove from the oven and let stand until completely cool. Wrap and chill before slicing.

Serves 8 to 10

Cream Cheese Pound Cake

This cake is golden, moist, and delicious.

1/2 cup (1 stick) butter, softened
1 cup (2 sticks) margarine, softened
8 ounces cream cheese, softened
3 cups sugar
6 eggs, at room temperature
3 cups cake flour
1 teaspoon vanilla extract

Beat the butter, margarine and cream cheese at medium speed in a mixing bowl for 1 to 7 minutes or until creamy. Add the sugar gradually, beating constantly until fluffy. Add the eggs one at a time, beating just until the yolk disappears after each addition. Add the cake flour gradually, beating constantly until blended. Do not overmix. Stir in the vanilla. Pour the batter evenly into a heavy bundt pan sprayed with nonstick cooking spray. Bake in a preheated 325-degree oven for 1 hour. Increase the oven temperature to 350 degrees. Bake for 10 to 15 minutes longer or until a wooden pick inserted in the center comes out clean. Do not overbake or the cake will be dry.

Serves 15

Red Velvet Cupcakes with Buttercream Frosting

Nancy Johnson • *Like No Other Bakery, Etc.*

These perfect high-altitude cupcakes are featured on the cover.

Cupcakes
1 (2-layer) package red velvet cake mix
4 eggs
1/2 cup vegetable oil
11/4 cups water
1/4 cup vanilla instant pudding mix
1/4 cup all-purpose flour

Buttercream Frosting
3/4 cup shortening
1/2 cup (1 stick) margarine, softened
1/8 teaspoon salt
2 tablespoons Torani vanilla syrup
2 tablespoons Torani chocolate
   biscotti syrup
11/2 pounds confectioners' sugar
1/4 cup milk

To prepare the cupcakes, combine the cake mix, eggs, oil, water, pudding mix and flour in a mixing bowl and beat at medium speed for 2 minutes. Fill twenty-four paper-lined muffin cups three-fourths full with batter. Bake in a preheated 350-degree oven for 15 to 18 minutes or until the cupcakes test done. Cool completely.

To prepare the frosting, beat the shortening, margarine and salt in a mixing bowl until blended, stopping to scrape down the side of the bowl. Add the syrups and beat at medium speed until smooth. Add half the confectioners' sugar and mix well. Add the milk gradually, beating constantly at high speed for 5 minutes. Add the remaining confectioners' sugar and beat at low speed until blended. Increase the speed to high and beat for 5 minutes. Scrape down the side of the bowl. Beat at high speed for 5 minutes longer. Frost the cooled cupcakes.

Makes 24 cupcakes

Polenta Shortcake

Alicia Prescott • *Executive Pastry Chef, The Blue Star and Nosh*

An amazing variation on the classic shortcake.

2 cups all-purpose flour, sifted
1/4 cup polenta
1/2 teaspoon baking powder
1 teaspoon salt
1/2 teaspoon baking soda
2 cups sugar
1 1/2 cups buttermilk
4 eggs
1/2 cup olive oil
Juice and zest of 1 lemon

Mix the flour, polenta, baking powder, salt and baking soda together. Whisk the sugar, buttermilk, eggs, olive oil, lemon juice and lemon zest in a large mixing bowl until mixed. Add the flour mixture and stir until smooth. Pour into a greased and floured bundt pan. Bake in a preheated 350-degree oven for 45 to 55 minutes or until golden brown and firm in the middle. Invert onto a sheet pan to cool. Cool completely before slicing to serve.

Serves 8

Cinnamon and Vanilla-Scented Peach and Raspberry Pie

1¹/2 cups fresh raspberries
3 pounds ripe peaches, peeled and cut into wedges
¹/2 cup granulated sugar
¹/3 cup packed light brown sugar
¹/3 cup all-purpose flour

¹/4 teaspoon cinnamon
1 vanilla bean pod, split lengthwise
2 refrigerator pie pastries
2 tablespoons whipping cream
1 to 2 tablespoons granulated sugar

Combine the raspberries, peaches, ¹/2 cup granulated sugar, the brown sugar, flour and cinnamon in a large bowl and toss to mix. Scrape the seeds from the vanilla bean pod into the fruit mixture and toss to mix. Let stand for 20 minutes.

Fit one pie pastry into a 9-inch glass pie plate, trimming the overhang to ¹/2 inch. Spoon the fruit mixture into the pastry-lined pie plate. Drape the remaining pie pastry over the top, trimming the overhang to ³/4 inch. Fold the edge of the top and bottom pastries under, pressing to seal. Crimp the edges decoratively and cut four to six vents in the top. Brush the pastry lightly with the whipping cream and sprinkle with 1 to 2 tablespoons granulated sugar. Place the pie on a baking sheet to catch drips. Bake in a preheated 400-degree oven for 45 minutes. Cover the crust to prevent overbrowning. Bake for 1 hour longer or until the juices bubble and the crust is golden brown. Cool completely on a wire rack.

Serves 8

Creamy Peanut Butter Pie

1¹/₂ cups crushed graham crackers
¹/₄ cup sugar
¹/₂ cup (1 stick) margarine, melted
²/₃ cup peanut butter

¹/₂ cup milk
1 cup confectioners' sugar
6 ounces cream cheese, softened
8 ounces whipped topping

Mix one-half of the graham cracker crumbs, the sugar and margarine in a bowl. Press into a 9-inch pie plate. Bake in a preheated 350-degree oven for 10 minutes. Remove from the oven to cool. Combine the peanut butter, milk, confectioners' sugar and cream cheese in a mixing bowl and mix until smooth. Fold in the whipped topping. Spoon into the cooled pie shell. Sprinkle with the remaining graham cracker crumbs. Freeze until firm.

Serves 8

Gooey Cocoa Chocolate Pudding Cake
Alicia Prescott • *Executive Pastry Chef, The Blue Star and Nosh*

Hot chocolate and Bailey's Irish cream are used to prepare this gooey chocolate cake.

1¹/₂ cups granulated sugar
2 cups plus 2 tablespoons
all-purpose flour
6 tablespoons baking cocoa
2 teaspoons baking powder
¹/₂ teaspoon salt
1 cup milk
10 tablespoons butter, softened

1 tablespoon vanilla extract
1 cup granulated sugar
¹/₂ cup baking cocoa
1 cup packed brown sugar
2¹/₂ cups hot chocolate
Splash of Bailey's Irish cream
Whipped cream or ice cream
Fresh berries

Mix 1¹/₂ cups granulated sugar, the flour, 6 tablespoons baking cocoa, the baking powder and salt in a mixing bowl. Add the milk, butter and vanilla and beat until smooth. Pour into a greased 9×13-inch metal cake pan.

Mix 1 cup granulated sugar, ¹/₂ cup baking cocoa and the brown sugar in a bowl. Sprinkle over the batter. Blend the hot chocolate and liqueur together and pour over the batter. Do not stir. Bake in a preheated 350-degree oven for 35 to 40 minutes or until the center is set. Let cool for 15 minutes. To serve, cut into squares and invert onto dessert plates or into bowls. Top with whipped cream and fresh berries.

Serves 8

Bread Pudding with Brandy Sauce

Bread Pudding
8 plain croissants, cubed
3/4 cup golden raisins
3 eggs
3/4 cup granulated sugar
1 1/4 cups milk
1 1/4 cups cream
2 tablespoons brandy
1/4 cup (1/2 stick) unsalted butter, melted
1 teaspoon cinnamon
1 teaspoon freshly ground nutmeg
1 teaspoon vanilla extract

Pinch of salt
1/4 cup (1/2 stick) butter
1 tablespoon cinnamon-sugar

Brandy Sauce
1 tablespoon cornstarch
1/4 cup (1/2 stick) butter
1 cup packed dark brown sugar
3/4 cup water
3/4 cup whipping cream
1 teaspoon vanilla extract
3 tablespoons brandy

To prepare the bread pudding, place one-half of the croissant cubes in a greased 9×11-inch baking dish. Sprinkle with the raisins. Top with the remaining croissant cubes. Beat the eggs in a mixing bowl until light. Add the sugar gradually, beating until thick. Whisk in the milk, cream, brandy, melted butter, cinnamon, nutmeg, vanilla and salt. Pour over the croissants. Chill, covered, for 1 hour or up to 24 hours until the liquid is absorbed. Bring to room temperature. Dot with 1/4 cup butter and sprinkle with the cinnamon-sugar. Bake, covered with foil, in a preheated 350-degree oven for 40 minutes.

To prepare the sauce, mix the cornstarch with a small amount of water in a small bowl to form a paste. Combine the butter, brown sugar and water in a small saucepan. Bring to a boil. Cook until the sugar is dissolved, stirring constantly. Add the cream, vanilla and cornstarch paste. Cook until thickened, stirring constantly. Stir in the brandy. Serve with the bread pudding.

Serves 16

*The brandy sauce can be made in advance
and reheated before serving.*

New York-Style Cheesecake with Chocolate Ganache Topping

The chocolate ganache makes this a divine dessert.

Cheesecake
1¹/2 cups graham cracker crumbs or chocolate sandwich cookie crumbs
¹/4 cup sugar
¹/4 cup (¹/2 stick) butter
32 ounces cream cheese, softened
1 (14-ounce) can sweetened condensed milk
4 eggs, at room temperature
¹/4 cup all-purpose flour
1 tablespoon vanilla extract

Chocolate Ganache Topping
1 cup heavy cream
12 ounces semisweet chocolate, chopped

To prepare the cheesecake, mix the graham cracker crumbs, sugar and butter in a bowl. Press into a springform pan. Chill in the refrigerator. If you use chocolate sandwich cookie crumbs for the crust, omit the sugar. Beat the cream cheese in a bowl until smooth. Add the condensed milk and mix well. Add the eggs one at a time, beating well after each addition and scraping down the side of the bowl. Add the flour and vanilla and mix well. Do not overmix. The total mixing time should take about 3 to 4 minutes. Pour the batter into the prepared springform pan. Wrap the outside of the springform pan in two layers of foil covering the bottom and side completely. Place in a larger baking pan and place on the middle oven rack. Add enough warm water to the larger pan to come halfway up the side of the springform pan. Bake in a preheated 325-degree or 350-degee oven for 40 to 50 minutes or until the center is set. Turn off the oven. Let stand in the oven for 30 to 60 minutes to prevent the cheesecake from cracking. Remove from the oven to the refrigerator. Chill for 4 to 10 hours so the cheesecake has time to set. Remove the foil from the springform pan and release the side of the pan. Place the cheesecake on a round cake board and place on a cooling rack on top of a baking sheet.

To prepare the topping, heat the cream in a small saucepan over medium to medium-low heat until slightly bubbly. Remove from the heat. Add the chocolate and stir until smooth and thick. If the topping is not thick enough, chill until thick but pourable, stirring occasionally. Pour over the top and side of the cheesecake, spreading evenly with a flat spatula. Chill for 1 hour or until set.

Serves 8 to 12

Lavender Crème Brûlée

Lavender, a member of the mint family, imbues this classic dessert with a floral taste and scent.

1¹/₂ cups heavy whipping cream
10 lavender flowers
6 egg yolks
¹/₂ cup granulated sugar
12 tablespoons brown sugar
Lavender or other edible flowers for garnish

Heat the cream and flowers in a small saucepan for 7 minutes. Do not boil. Remove from the heat. Let stand for 30 minutes to allow the lavender to infuse the cream. Strain the cream through a sieve into a bowl to remove the lavender flowers. Let stand until cool. Whisk the egg yolks and granulated sugar in a bowl until smooth. Whisk in the lavender-infused cream gradually. Pour into six individual ovenproof ramekins. Arrange in a 9×13-inch baking pan. Pour enough hot water into the baking pan to come halfway up the side of the ramekins. Bake in a preheated 325-degree oven for 40 minutes or until set. Remove from the oven. Let stand in the water bath for 30 minutes to cool. Remove from the water bath and chill for 8 to 10 hours. This may be prepared up to a day before serving.

Preheat a broiler. Sprinkle 2 tablespoons brown sugar over the top of each custard. Broil for 2 to 3 minutes or until the brown sugar is caramelized. Let stand to cool completely or chill for up to 30 minutes. Garnish with lavender flowers.

Serves 6

Chocolate Raspberry or Hazelnut Truffles

Alicia Prescott • *Executive Pastry Chef, The Blue Star and Nosh*

These are a delicious and easy holiday gift or party idea, and it's fun to get the family involved.

1$\frac{1}{2}$ pounds dark chocolate chips
12 ounces milk chocolate chips
10 ounces heavy cream
$\frac{1}{2}$ cup (1 stick) unsalted butter, cut into cubes
3 tablespoons raspberry liqueur, hazelnut liqueur or favorite liqueur

Melt the chocolate chips in a double boiler. Bring the cream and butter to a boil in a saucepan. Pour into the chocolate and stir until smooth. Stir in the liqueur. Chill thoroughly. Scoop into balls using a small ice cream scoop or melon baller. The truffles can be rolled in baking cocoa, toasted crushed nuts, coconut or crushed hard candy such as peppermints.

Makes 100 truffles

*Three tablespoons liqueur will lightly flavor the chocolate.
Add more for a stronger flavor. Flavored extracts can also be substituted
for the liqueur. If the mixture becomes too chilled, it will be hard to
scoop. Let stand at room temperature until it is easier to scoop.*

Basil Jalapeño Mojito Sorbet

Serve as a dessert on a hot summer night—or as a palate cleanser just before a main entrée.

1 cup sugar
$^1/_2$ cup lemon-lime soda
20 fresh basil leaves
1 jalapeño chile, seeds and veins removed
3 tablespoons lime zest
$^3/_4$ cup fresh lime juice
20 fresh mint leaves
Sprigs of fresh basil and mint for garnish

Boil the sugar and soda in a saucepan until the sugar dissolves, stirring frequently. Remove from the heat and cool for 15 minutes. Purée the basil, jalapeño chile, lime zest, lime juice and mint in a food processor or blender. Add the sugar mixture and purée. Strain through a fine sieve into a bowl for a smooth texture; don't strain if you prefer a chunkier texture. Chill, covered, for 4 hours.

Pour into an ice cream freezer container. Freeze using the manufacturer's directions. Spoon into a plastic container. Freeze, covered, for 4 hours. To serve, scoop with a melon baller or small ice cream scoop into balls. Place one to three balls per serving in a dessert dish. Garnish with sprigs of basil and mint.

Makes 2 cups

Lemon Raspberry Vacherins
Barry Dunlap • *Executive Chef, Summit Catering*

These lemon meringue delights can be topped with any seasonal fresh berries.

Meringue Cups
3 egg whites, at room temperature
1/4 teaspoon cream of tartar
3/4 cup sugar

Lemon Curd
Zest and juice of 4 lemons
4 eggs
3/4 cup sugar
3/4 cup (1 1/2 sticks) unsalted butter,
    cut into cubes
Fresh raspberries for topping

To prepare the meringue cups, beat the egg whites in a mixing bowl for 1 minute or until frothy. Add the cream of tartar and beat for 1 minute or until soft peaks form. Add the sugar gradually, beating for 3 to 6 minutes or until stiff peaks form. Spoon into a piping bag fitted with a 1/4-inch plain tip. Line a baking sheet with baking parchment, placing a dab of the meringue under each corner to hold the baking parchment in place. Pipe 1/2-inch discs on the prepared pan, adding two spiraled rows around the outside of each disc to form a meringue cup. Place on the top rack in a preheated 300-degree oven and turn off the oven. Let stand in the oven for 8 to 10 hours to dry.

To prepare the lemon curd, place the lemon zest and lemon juice in a stainless steel saucepan. Beat the eggs and sugar in a mixing bowl until pale yellow. Stir into the juice mixture. Heat just until the mixture boils around the edge, stirring frequently. Stir in the butter until smooth. Strain into a bowl. Chill, covered, for up to 2 weeks.

To serve, pipe or spoon the lemon curd into the meringue cups. Top with fresh raspberries.

Serves 6 to 8

*The meringues can be made a day or two ahead of time
as can the lemon curd. For single servings, make the meringues
3 inches in diameter. For bite-size servings, make the
meringues 1/2 inch in diameter.*

Autumn Apple Crisp

*The crisp tastes incredible on its own and is even better when topped with
vanilla ice cream or whipped cream.*

2/3 cup all-purpose flour

3/4 cup packed brown sugar

1/4 cup chopped pecans or walnuts

1/4 teaspoon salt

1/2 teaspoon nutmeg

1/2 teaspoon cinnamon

6 tablespoons butter, cut into
1/2-inch pieces

5 or 6 large apples, peeled and chopped

2 tablespoons packed brown sugar

1 tablespoon lemon juice

1 teaspoon cinnamon

Whisk the flour, 3/4 cup brown sugar, the pecans, salt, nutmeg and 1/2 teaspoon cinnamon in a large mixing bowl of a stand mixer. Add the butter and beat with the paddle attachment or until the butter pieces are coated and the remaining mixture is coarse and crumbly. (The mixture can also be mixed with your fingers.)

Place the apples in a 2- to 2 1/2-quart gratin dish 2 inches tall. Add 2 tablespoons brown sugar, the lemon juice and 1 teaspoon cinnamon and toss gently to coat the apples. Cover the top with the crumb mixture. Place on a baking sheet to catch any drips. Bake on the middle rack in a preheated 375-degree oven for 30 to 45 minutes or until the apples are tender, the juices are bubbling and the top is golden brown.

Serves 6

*Once cooled, the apple crisp can be stored, covered, at room
temperature for up to 2 days. Reheat in a preheated 250-degree
oven for 15 minutes or in the microwave. The crisp is also good cold.*

Palisade Peaches Foster

Jerad Dody • *Executive Chef, moZaic Restaurant at the Inn at Palmer Divide*

*Palisade, Colorado, which is often called the "Heart of Colorado's Fruit and
Wine Country," is world famous for its peaches.*

2 tablespoons butter
1/2 cup packed brown sugar
6 Palisade peaches, peeled and sliced
1 teaspoon vanilla extract
1/2 teaspoon cinnamon
1/4 teaspoon nutmeg
1 tablespoon orange zest
2 tablespoons pecan pieces
1/2 cup Bacardi 151 dark rum
1/4 cup peach brandy
6 scoops of vanilla ice cream

Melt the butter with the brown sugar in a heavy sauté pan over medium heat until the brown sugar is completely dissolved. Add the peaches, vanilla, cinnamon, nutmeg and orange zest. Stir in the pecans. Flambé with the rum and then the brandy, using a long match and making sure to stand back. After the flames subside, spoon over the ice cream.

Serves 6

Peppered Strawberries

Lawrence "Chip" Johnson • *Proprietor and Executive Chef,*
The Warehouse Restaurant and Gallery

Flavored with sambuca and Cointreau, these strawberries are delightful when
spooned over vanilla ice cream.

3 cups strawberries

2/3 cup sugar

1/2 cup sambuca

1/4 cup Cointreau

2 teaspoons freshly ground pepper

1/3 cup heavy whipping cream

3 cups French vanilla ice cream

Cut the strawberries into thirds or quarters lengthwise and place in a bowl. Add the sugar and stir to coat. Stir in the liqueurs. Add the pepper and whipping cream and stir lightly. Spoon over the ice cream.

Serves 6

Vegan Banana Bread

This quick bread is made without butter or eggs and has a wonderful taste and texture.

3 ripe bananas

3 tablespoons olive oil

2 cups all-purpose flour

1/2 cup sugar

1 teaspoon salt

1 teaspoon baking soda

1/2 cup chopped walnuts

1 teaspoon vanilla extract

Cinnamon to taste

Vanilla or regular soy milk as needed

Mix the bananas, olive oil, flour, sugar, salt, baking soda, walnuts, vanilla and cinnamon in a large bowl with a spatula, adding a splash of soy milk if the mixture is dry. The batter will not be runny like most banana bread batter. Spoon into a greased 5×9-inch loaf pan. Bake in a preheated 350-degree oven for 1 hour or until a knife inserted in the center comes out clean.

Serves 8 to 10

Spiced Pumpkin Bread

This recipe makes three loaves, so be sure to share.

1^1/$_2$ cups granulated sugar	3^1/$_3$ cups all-purpose flour
1^1/$_2$ cups packed brown sugar	2 teaspoons baking soda
1 cup vegetable oil or canola oil	^{1}/$_2$ teaspoon ground cloves
4 eggs	1^1/$_2$ teaspoons salt
^{1}/$_3$ cup water	1^1/$_2$ teaspoons ginger
2 cups pumpkin (16 ounces)	1 tablespoon cinnamon

Combine the granulated sugar, brown sugar, oil, eggs and water in a mixing bowl and beat well. Add the pumpkin and mix well. Add the flour, baking soda, cloves, salt, ginger and cinnamon and mix well. Pour into three greased 4×8-inch metal loaf pans. Bake in a preheated 350-degree oven for 1 hour or until a wooden pick inserted in the center comes out clean. Invert onto a wire rack to cool.

Makes 3 loaves

The loaves can be baked in glass loaf dishes for 30 to 35 minutes or until the loaves test done.

Double Chocolate Zucchini Bread

This bread is a chocolate lover's delight.

4 cups all-purpose flour	3 eggs
1/2 cup baking cocoa	1 1/4 cups vegetable oil
1 cup granulated sugar	1 1/4 cups milk
1/2 cup packed brown sugar	2 teaspoons vanilla extract
2 teaspoons baking soda	2 cups grated zucchini
1/2 teaspoon baking powder	1 cup (6 ounces) semisweet
3/4 teaspoon salt	chocolate chips
1 teaspoon cinnamon	1/4 cup toffee bits (optional)
1/2 teaspoon nutmeg	1/4 cup walnut pieces (optional)

Whisk the flour, baking cocoa, granulated sugar, brown sugar, baking soda, baking powder, salt, cinnamon and nutmeg in a large bowl until mixed. Whisk the eggs, oil, milk and vanilla in a bowl until blended. Stir in the zucchini. Fold into the flour mixture just until mixed. Do not overmix. The batter will be chunky. Fold in the chocolate chips, toffee bits and walnut pieces. Pour into two buttered 4×8-inch loaf pans. Bake in a preheated 350-degree oven for 65 minutes or until a wooden pick inserted in the center comes out clean or with moist crumbs. (When testing for doneness, insert the wooden pick in several areas of the bread, because if you happen to hit a chocolate chip, the wooden pick will come out looking like uncooked batter or melted chocolate.) Cool in the pans on a wire rack for 20 minutes. Invert onto the wire rack to cool completely. Cut into slices with a serrated knife.

Makes 2 loaves

Do not use a mixer in this recipe because overmixing can cause the bread to be tough. For Triple Chocolate Zucchini Bread, add 1/2 cup (3 ounces) bittersweet chocolate chips.

Pineapple Cranberry Carrot Cake Muffins

Ground flaxseed adds omega-3 essential fatty acids to these morning muffins.

3 cups whole wheat flour
2 tablespoons ground flaxseed
1¼ teaspoons baking soda
1½ teaspoons baking powder
1 teaspoon salt
1½ teaspoons cinnamon
¼ teaspoon nutmeg
2 to 3 cups finely grated carrots
(about 3 or 4 carrots)

¾ cup dried cranberries
1¼ cups honey or pure maple syrup
(not pancake syrup)
1 cup canola oil
1 (20-ounce) can crushed
pineapple, drained
1 teaspoon vanilla extract
3 eggs, lightly beaten
1½ cups pecan pieces

Mix the whole wheat flour, flaxseed, baking soda, baking powder, salt, cinnamon and nutmeg together. Combine the carrots, cranberries, honey, canola oil, pineapple, vanilla and eggs in a bowl and mix well. Add the whole wheat flour mixture and stir just until moistened. Stir in the pecan pieces. Spoon into paper-lined muffin cups, filling two-thirds full. Bake in a preheated 350-degree oven for 25 minutes. Invert onto a wire rack. Serve warm.

Makes 24

*To grind flaxseed, wipe out the inside top and bottom of
an electric coffee grinder with a dry paper towel.
Pour the flaxseed into the coffee grinder and grind until powdery.
The flaxseed is then ready to add to the dry ingredients.*

Cranberry and White Chocolate Scones

The orange juice glaze drizzled over these scones adds a wonderful citrus taste.

Scones
2 cups all-purpose flour
2 teaspoons baking powder
3 tablespoons sugar
1/2 teaspoon salt
3/4 cup (11/2 sticks) salted butter
1/2 cup dried cranberries
6 ounces white chocolate chips
1/2 cup half-and-half

Orange Glaze
3 tablespoons confectioners' sugar
2 tablespoons orange juice

To prepare the scones, line a baking sheet with foil and spray with nonstick cooking spray. Mix the flour, baking powder, sugar and salt in a bowl. Cut in the butter until crumbly. Add the cranberries and white chocolate chips. Add the half-and-half and stir to form a crumbly ball. Knead 10 times on a lightly floured surface. Divide the dough into two equal portions. Shape each portion into a ball. Press each ball into a circle 1/2 inch thick. Cut into wedges and place on the prepared baking sheet. Bake in a preheated 400-degree oven for 15 minutes.

To prepare the glaze, mix the confectioners' sugar and orange juice in a bowl until smooth. Drizzle over the scones.

Serves 8

Banana Muffin Spice Cookies

These cookies are soft and have a muffin-like consistency.

Cookies
2 cups all-purpose flour
2 teaspoons baking powder
1/4 teaspoon baking soda
1/4 teaspoon salt
1/2 teaspoon cinnamon
1/4 teaspoon ground cloves
1/2 cup chopped nuts
1/2 cup (1 stick) butter, softened
1 cup packed brown sugar

2 eggs
1 cup mashed bananas (2 or 3 bananas)

Vanilla Frosting
1 cup sifted confectioners' sugar
1/4 teaspoon salt
1/2 teaspoon vanilla extract
1 1/2 tablespoons water, or
    4 1/2 tablespoons cream

To prepare the cookies, mix the flour, baking powder, baking soda, salt, cinnamon, cloves and nuts together. Combine the butter, brown sugar and eggs in a mixing bowl and mix well. Stir in the bananas. Add the flour mixture and mix well. Chill the dough for 1 hour. Drop by teaspoonfuls 2 inches apart onto a lightly greased cookie sheet. Bake in a preheated 375-degree oven for 8 to 10 minutes or until brown. Cool on a wire rack.

To prepare the frosting, mix the confectioners' sugar, salt, vanilla and water in a bowl until of a spreading consistency. Spread over the cookies.

Makes 3 to 4 dozen

*Lemon, almond, or peppermint flavoring can be used instead
of the vanilla extract in the frosting.*

Chocolate Coconut Oatmeal Cookies

These cookies are a crowd pleaser, which is good since this recipe makes six dozen cookies.

4 cups all-purpose flour
2 cups shredded coconut
4 cups quick-cooking oats
2 teaspoons salt
2 teaspoons baking soda
2 teaspoons baking powder
2 cups chopped nuts
2 cups (12 ounces) chocolate chips
2 cups packed brown sugar
2 cups granulated sugar
2 cups (4 sticks) butter, chilled
4 eggs
4 teaspoons vanilla extract

Mix the flour, coconut, oats, salt, baking soda, baking powder, nuts and chocolate chips together in a large bowl. Combine the brown sugar, granulated sugar, butter, eggs and vanilla in a large mixing bowl and beat well. Add the flour mixture gradually, stirring well after each addition. Drop by spoonfuls onto a cookie sheet lined with baking parchment. Bake in a preheated 375-degree oven for 10 to 12 minutes or until brown. Cool on a wire rack.

Makes 6 dozen

Southwest Spiced Chocolate Chip Cookies

Cayenne pepper, chocolate, and pine nuts give these cookies a southwestern flair.

$1/2$ cup shortening
$1/2$ cup (1 stick) butter, softened
$1/2$ cup granulated sugar
1 cup packed brown sugar
$1/2$ teaspoon baking soda
2 eggs
1 teaspoon vanilla extract
1 teaspoon cinnamon
$1/4$ teaspoon nutmeg
$1/8$ teaspoon ground cloves
1 pinch of cayenne pepper (optional)
$2^1/2$ cups all-purpose flour
8 ounces milk chocolate chips
$1/2$ cup pine nuts, toasted
$1/2$ cup sliced almonds

Cream the shortening and butter in a mixing bowl until light and fluffy. Add the granulated sugar, brown sugar and baking soda and beat well, scraping the side of the bowl occasionally. Beat in the eggs and vanilla. Beat in the cinnamon, nutmeg, cloves, cayenne pepper and flour. Stir in the chocolate chips, pine nuts and almonds. Chill the dough for 1 to 2 hours. Drop the dough by rounded teaspoonfuls 2 inches apart onto an ungreased cookie sheet. Bake in a preheated 375-degree oven for 8 to 10 minutes or until the edges are light brown. Remove to a wire rack to cool.

Makes 4 to 5 dozen

Contributors

This cookbook is a collaboration and could not have been accomplished without the time and talents of many people. Special thank you to all of The Junior League of Colorado Springs members, families, and friends who contributed, prepared, and tasted recipes, hosted tasting events, and helped make this cookbook a success. We apologize if we have inadvertently omitted any names.

Alissa Aguilar
Sherri L. Albertson
Carolyn Allen
Lisa Alvernaz
Courtney Arnstein
Jim Arnstein
Tricia Asp
Ken Barker
Gwen Barron
Cyndi Baumgardner
Jenny Bender
Zack Bender
Jessica Bennett
Kirk Bigger
Melissa Blevins
Robert Blevins
Jean Bodman
Alyssa Boswell
Allisyn Booth
Ann Bowman
Emily Boyes
Anne Bradley
Trish Brock
Al Buettner
Leigh Buettner

Nancy Bunker
Steve Caudle
Laurie Carlstrom
Jennifer Clarke
Patricia B. Cole
Ruth S. Connell
Mary Frances Cowan
Mia Crane
Andrew T. Darrigan
Ann Davenport
James W. Davis, Jr.
Maria Dempsey
Tina Dewar
Jerad Dody
Laura Dreher
Barry Dunlap
Melissa Emerick
Gary Feffer
Kim Feffer
Tricia Flood
Sandy Forrest
Craig Foster
Lisa Fry
Stephanie Goodwin
Shelia Greene

Carol A. Gugat
Rebecca Hane
Kim Hanou
Bethany Hanson
Amy Harder
Jill Hare
April Harker
Megan Harmon
Andrene Harris
Janell Harvey
Nadine Hensler
Anna Houser
Eric Howard
Lisa Howard
Cindy Huff
Rachel Jervis
Lawrence "Chip" Johnson
Nancy Johnson
Paula Johnson
Luke Jones
Natalie Jones
Cari Karns
Judy Kendall
Joan Kenney
Shawna Kerran

Contributors

Tyler Kerran
Molly Kinne
Marigny Klaber
Chana Kolman
Sharon Laahs
Jenny Ladra
Lori Langin
Austin Haggard Lawhorn
Jami Leahy
Deonna Lechner
Suzanne Lee
Page Lewis
Katherine Looney
Joy Love
Sarah Lueckeman
Yolanda Lyons
Sheron Marshall
Tessa Martinez
Britny Massey
Vickie Mathers-Stauffer
Cathy Michopoulos
Trisha Miller
Rebecca Morris
Cheryl Murphy
Tracey Muterspaugh
Marne O'Brien-Hillis
Andrea Pacheco
Jennifer Parris
Muriel Pearce Ostien

Lynn Pelz
Jonathan Peterson
Lindsae Phillips
Hartley Pohjola
Felicia Popowski
Rebecca Post
Alicia Prescott
Jessica Raab
Beth Rawley
Shannon Rawley
Yani Rehorn
Melanie Reynolds
Sara Richards
Susan Richards
Paige Robers
Marilyn Roberts
Alexis Rodman
Shannon Rowe
Alicia Rule
Diane Rutherford
Lynette Ryden
Brian Sack
Tyler Sanders
Cherish Schaffer
Lisa Scott
Lauré Secker
Walker Secker
Erica Scott
Ashley Seiler

Erin Smiley
B. Thomas Smith
Mary Ellis Smith
Vickie Smith
Greg Soukup
Megghan St. Aubyn
Aimee Stephenson
Amber Strang
Betty Street
Pamela Street
Catherine Taryle
Terry Thatcher
Lauri Thomas
Sarah Thompson
Nichole Tipton
Kristopher Trumble
Alice Varalli
Elizabeth Venner
Katherine Walrod
Barbie Walsh
Bill Walsh
Elaine Whitt
Cathy Wilkins
Helen Wilkins
Krista Willard
Jennifer Williams
Lauren Witt
Susan Zimmerman

Index

Index

Index

Index

To purchase additional copies of
A Peak at the Springs,
or for more information, visit us on line at
www.jlcoloradosprings.org,
or call the Junior League of Colorado Springs
at 719-632-3855.